OS X® MOUNTAIN LION

Simplified®

Visual

by **Paul McFedries**

D1456722

WILEY

John Wiley & Sons, Inc.

OS X® MOUNTAIN LION SIMPLIFIED®

Published by
John Wiley & Sons, Inc.
10475 Crosspoint Boulevard
Indianapolis, IN 46256

www.wiley.com

Published simultaneously in Canada

Copyright © 2012 by John Wiley & Sons, Inc., Indianapolis, Indiana

Wiley publishes in a variety of print and electronic formats and by print-on-demand. Some material included with standard print versions of this book may not be included in e-books or in print-on-demand. If this book refers to media such as a CD or DVD that is not included in the version you purchased, you may download this material at http://booksupport.wiley.com. For more information about Wiley products, visit www.wiley.com.

Library of Congress Control Number: 2012948268

ISBN: 978-1-118-40141-5

Manufactured in the United States of America

10 9 8 7 6 5 4 3 2 1

Trademark Acknowledgments

Contact Us

For general information on our other products and services please contact our Customer Care Department within the U.S. at 877-762-2974, outside the U.S. at 317-572-3993 or fax 317-572-4002.

For technical support please visit www.wiley.com/techsupport.

WILEY

John Wiley & Sons, Inc.

Sales
Contact Wiley at (877) 762-2974 or fax (317) 572-4002.

Credits

Acquisitions Editor
Aaron Black

Project Editor
Jade L. Williams

Technical Editor
Dennis Cohen

Copy Editor
Marylouise Wiack

Editorial Director
Robyn Siesky

Business Manager
Amy Knies

Senior Marketing Manager
Sandy Smith

Vice President and Executive Group Publisher
Richard Swadley

Vice President and Executive Publisher
Barry Pruett

Senior Project Coordinator
Kristie Rees

Graphics and Production Specialists
Anna Carillo
Joyce Haughey
Jennifer Henry
Andrea Hornberger
Jennifer Mayberry
Jill A. Proll

Quality Control Technician
John Greenough

Proofreading
The Well-Chosen Word

Indexing
Potomac Indexing, LLC

About the Author

Paul McFedries is is a technical writer who has been authoring computer books since 1991. He has more than 75 books to his credit, which together have sold more than four million copies worldwide. These books include the Wiley titles *Teach Yourself VISUALLY Macs, Third Edition*, *MacBook Air Portable Genius, Third Edition*, *iPhone 4S Portable Genius*, and *The new iPad Portable Genius*. Paul also runs Word Spy, a website dedicated to tracking new words and phrases (see www.wordspy.com). You may visit Paul's personal website at www.mcfedries.com, or follow him on twitter at www.twitter.com/paulmcf and www.twitter.com/wordspy.

Author's Acknowledgments

The book you hold in your hands is not only an excellent learning tool, but it is truly beautiful, as well. I am happy to have supplied the text that you will read, but the beautiful layout and colors come from Wiley's crack team of graphics specialists and illustrators. The scope of the tasks, the accuracy of the spelling and grammar, and the veracity of the information are all the result of hard work performed by project editor Jade Williams, copy editor Marylouise Wiack, and technical editor Dennis Cohen. Thanks to all of you for your excellent work. My thanks, as well, to acquisitions editor Aaron Black for asking me to write this book.

How to Use This Book

Who This Book Is For

This book is for the reader who has never used this particular technology or software application. It is also for readers who want to expand their knowledge.

The Conventions in This Book

1 Steps

This book uses a step-by-step format to guide you easily through each task. Numbered steps are actions you must do; bulleted steps clarify a point, step, or optional feature; and indented steps give you the result.

2 Notes

Notes give additional information — special conditions that may occur during an operation, a situation that you want to avoid, or a cross reference to a related area of the book.

3 Icons and Buttons

Icons and buttons show you exactly what you need to click to perform a step.

4 Simplify It

Simplify It sections offer additional information, including warnings and shortcuts.

5 Bold

Bold type shows command names, options, and text or numbers you must type.

6 Italics

Italic type introduces and defines a new term.

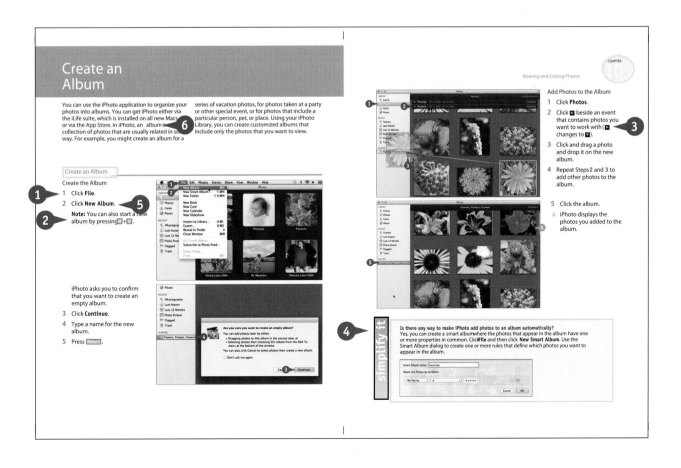

Table of Contents

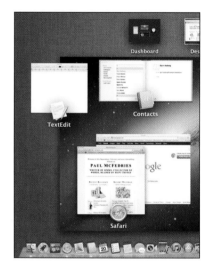

Table of Contents

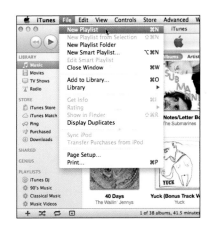

Table of Contents

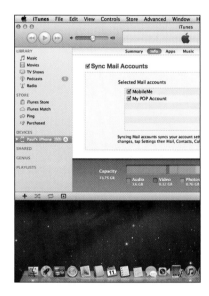

CHAPTER 1

Reviewing What You Can Do with OS X

Are you ready to learn about what you can do with OS X? In this chapter, you find out about the wide variety of tasks you can perform with OS X. These tasks include creating documents, spreadsheets, and presentations; playing, importing, and purchasing music; importing, organizing, and editing photos and videos; surfing the web; communicating with others via e-mail, messages, and video calls; and working with contacts and appointments.

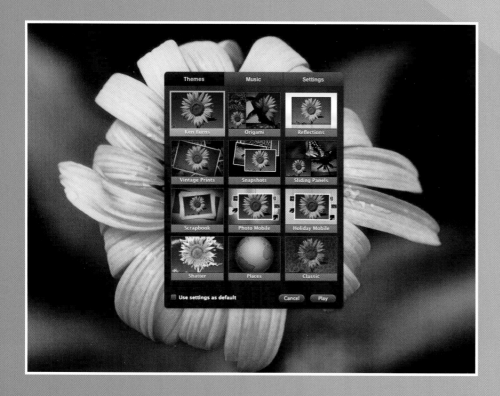

Create Documents

Whether you use your Mac at home, at the office, or on the road, you can use OS X to create a wide variety of documents. In general, terms, a *document* is a file that contains information, which is usually text, but it may also consist of pictures, charts, lines, and other nontext items. With OS X, you can create documents such as lists, letters, memos, budgets, forecasts, presentations, and web pages.

Text Documents

You can use text-editing software on OS X to create simple documents such as lists, notes, instructions, and other items that do not require fonts, colors, or other types of formatting. With OS X, you can use the TextEdit application to create plain text documents, and the Stickies application to create electronic sticky notes.

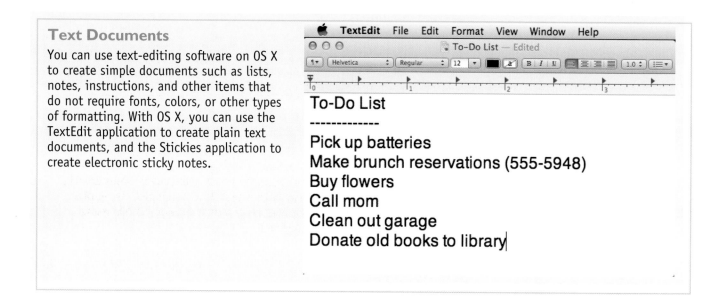

Word Processing Documents

You can use word processing software on OS X to create letters, resumes, memos, reports, newsletters, brochures, business cards, menus, flyers, invitations, and certificates. Anything that you use to communicate on paper, you can create using OS X. You can also use TextEdit to create formatted documents. Other examples include Microsoft Word for the Mac and Apple iWork Pages.

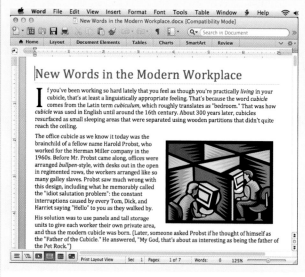

Spreadsheets

A spreadsheet application is a software program that enables you to manipulate numbers and formulas to quickly create powerful mathematical, financial, and statistical models. OS X comes with a test drive version of the Apple iWork Numbers application. Another example is Microsoft Excel for the Mac.

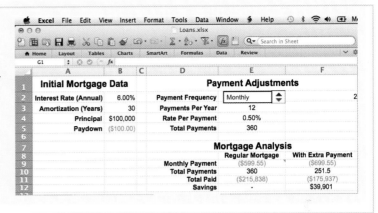

Presentations

A presentation program enables you to build professional-looking slides that you can use to convey your ideas to other people. OS X comes with a test drive version of the Apple iWork Keynote application. Another example is Microsoft PowerPoint for the Mac.

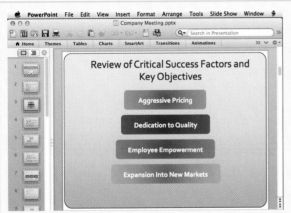

Web Pages

You can use web-page editing software on OS X to create your own pages to publish to the web. You can create a personal home page, a blog, or pages to support your business. OS X does not come with a program for creating Web pages, but the App Store contains several excellent apps, including TextWrangler, BBEdit, and Web Form Builder Lite.

Play and Record Music

OS X is a veritable music machine that you can use to build, organize, play, and share your digital music collection. You can get music onto your Mac by copying it from audio CDs, or by purchasing music online. If you are musically inclined, you can record or compose new tunes using an application called GarageBand (part of the Apple iLife suite). After you have a collection of music on your Mac, you can use OS X to create custom music CDs, or copy some or all of the music to a device such as an iPod or iPad.

iTunes

OS X comes with the iTunes application, which stores your library of digital music files. With iTunes, you can play albums and songs, organize tunes into related playlists, download and edit track information, and organize your music to suit your style. You can also use iTunes to listen to Internet-based radio stations.

iTunes Store

You can use the iTunes application to connect directly to the online iTunes Store, where you can purchase individual songs, usually for 99 cents per song, or entire albums, usually for $9.99 per album. OS X downloads the purchased music to your iTunes library, and you can listen to the music on your Mac or add the music to your iPod, iPhone, or iPad.

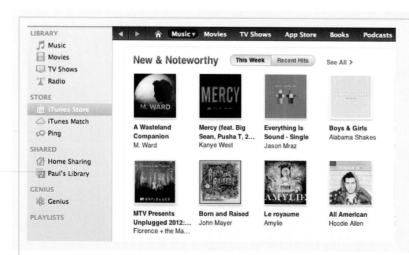

Import Music from a CD

You can add tracks from a music CD to the iTunes library. This enables you to listen to an album without having to put the CD into your CD or DVD drive each time. In iTunes, the process of copying tracks from a CD to your Mac is called *importing* or *ripping*.

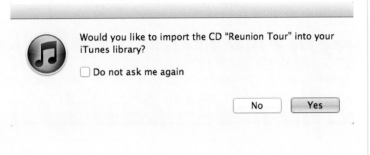

Record Music

If your Mac came with the iLife suite, then you can use the GarageBand program to record or compose your own tunes. You can attach an instrument such as a guitar or keyboard to your Mac and record your playing. You can also use GarageBand to add accompanying instruments such as drums, bass, piano, or another guitar.

Burn Music to a CD

You can copy, or *burn*, music files from your Mac onto a CD. Burning CDs is a great way to create customized CDs that you can listen to on the computer or in a portable device. You can burn music files using the iTunes application.

Synchronize with an iPod, iPhone, or iPad

You can use the iTunes application to copy some or all your music library to an iPod, iPhone, or iPad; this enables you to play your music wherever you are or on another audio device that connects to the device. When you attach the iPod, iPhone, or iPad to your Mac, iTunes automatically synchronizes the device according to the settings you specify.

View and Organize Your Photos

Your Mac is perfect for showing your digital photos in their best light. OS X comes with tools that enable you to view individual photos and to run slide shows of multiple photos. OS X also enables you to organize your digital photos, import images from a digital camera or similar device (such as an iPhone or iPad), and edit your photos. Many Macs also come with a built-in camera that you can use to take simple snapshots.

View Photos

OS X gives you many ways to view your digital photos. You can view photos within Finder using the Cover Flow view, or by selecting the photos and pressing `Spacebar`. You can also double-click a photo file to open it using the Preview application, or you can open a file using the iPhoto application, if it is installed on your Mac. Also, both Preview and iPhoto enable you to run photo slide shows.

Organize Photos

If your Mac comes with iPhoto, part of the Apple iLife suite, you can use it to organize your collection of digital photos. For example, you can create albums of related photos, and you can create folders in which to store photos. You can also rename and rate photos, apply keywords to photos, flag important photos, and sort photos in various ways.

Import Photos to OS X

If you have a digital camera attached to your Mac, you can use either the Image Capture application or the iPhoto application, part of the Apple iLife suite, to import some or all of the camera's images to OS X.

Take Snapshots

If your Mac includes an iSight camera or has a digital video camera connected, you can use the Photo Booth application to take snapshots of whatever subject is currently displayed in the camera. You can also apply various effects to the photos.

Edit Photos

If your Mac comes with the iPhoto application, you can use it to edit your digital photos. You can rotate, crop, or straighten a photo; you can modify a photo's exposure, contrast, and sharpness; you can fix problems such as red eye and blemishes; and you can apply special effects to a photo.

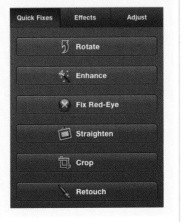

Play and Make a Movie or Slide Show

Your Mac's solid graphical underpinnings mean that it is a great tool for video playback. For example, OS X comes with tools that enable you to watch movies on DVD. You can play digital video such as movies, TV shows, and podcast files that you download from the Internet, or digital video that you import from a camera. You can also use OS X to create your own digital movies and your own photo slide shows.

Play a DVD

If your Mac has a DVD drive, you can use the DVD Player application to play a DVD movie. You can either use full-screen mode to watch the movie using the entire screen, or watch the movie in a window while you work on other things. DVD Player has features that enable you to control the movie playback and volume.

Play a Video File

OS X comes with an application called QuickTime Player that enables you to open video files and control the playback and volume. QuickTime Player also includes many extra features, including the ability to record movies and audio, cut and paste scenes, and publish your videos on services such as YouTube and Facebook.

Play a Movie, TV Show, or Podcast

You most often use iTunes to play music, but you can also use it to play movies, video files stored on your Mac, and TV shows that you purchase from the iTunes Store, as well as podcasts that you download from the iTunes Store or subscribe to online.

Make a Movie

Most Macs come with an application called iMovie, part of the Apple iLife suite, which enables you to make your own digital movies. You can import clips from a video camera or video file, add clips to the movie, and rearrange and trim those clips as needed. You can also add transitions between scenes, music and sound effects, titles, and more.

Make a Slide Show

You can use OS X to create your own photo slide shows. Using the iPhoto application, part of the Apple iLife suite, you can create a slide show of your photos that includes animation effects, transition effects, and music. You can enhance the slide show with photo titles and sophisticated background and text themes.

Take Advantage of the Web

You can use OS X to connect to your Internet account. Once the connection has been established, you can use the built-in web browser to access almost any site that is available on the web. This means you can use your Mac to search for information, read the latest news, research and purchase goods and services, sell your own items, socialize with others, and more.

Surf the Web

OS X comes with a browser application called Safari that you use to surf the web. Safari offers several ways to load and navigate web pages. You can also use Safari to save your favorite web pages as bookmarks, view multiple pages in a single window using tabs, download files to your Mac, and much more.

Search for Information

If you need information on a specific topic, free websites called *search engines* enable you to quickly search the web for pages that have the information you require. You can search the web either by going directly to a search engine site or by using the search feature built into Safari.

Read News

The web is home to many sites that enable you to read the latest news. For example, many print sources have websites, some magazines exist only online, and there are more recent innovations such as blogs and RSS feeds. Some media sites require that you register to access the articles, but on most sites, the registration is free.

Buy and Sell

e-Commerce — the online buying and selling of goods and services — is a big part of the web. You can use web-based stores to purchase books, theater tickets, and even cars, which gives you the convenience of shopping at home, easily comparing prices and features, and having goods delivered to your door. Many sites also enable you to sell or auction your products or household items.

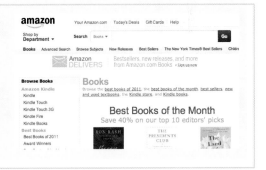

Socialize

The web offers many opportunities to socialize, whether you are looking for a friend or a date, or you just want some good conversation. However, it is a good idea to observe some common-sense precautions. For example, arrange to meet new friends in public places, supervise all online socializing done by children, and do not give out personal information to strangers.

Take Advantage of iCloud

You can use OS X to set up a free web-based iCloud account that enables you to perform many activities online, including exchanging e-mail, maintaining contacts, and tracking appointments. You can also use your iCloud account to synchronize data between your Mac and other Macs, Windows PCs, and devices such as iPods, iPhones, and iPads.

Communicate with Others

You can use OS X to communicate with other people using online and wireless technologies. For example, once you have connected your Mac to the Internet, you can start sending and receiving e-mail, using either your Internet service provider (ISP) account or a web-based account. You can also use your Internet connection to exchange instant messages and perform audio and video chats. If you have a camera attached to your Mac, you can also place video calls to other people through your wired or wireless network.

Exchange E-mail

E-mail is the Internet system that enables you to electronically exchange messages with other Internet users anywhere in the world. To use e-mail, you must have an e-mail account, which is usually supplied by your ISP or e-mail service. The account gives you an e-mail address to which others can send messages. You then set up that account in the OS X Mail application.

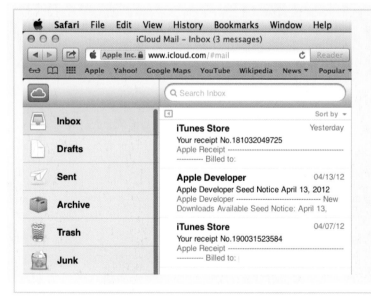

Exchange E-mail over the Web

You can also set up a web-based e-mail account. Although you can do this using services such as Hotmail.com and Yahoo.com, many Mac users create iCloud accounts, which include web-based e-mail. A web-based account is convenient because it enables you to send and receive messages from any computer that has access to the Internet.

Exchange Instant Messages

Instant messaging allows you to contact other people who are online, thus enabling you to have a real-time exchange of messages. Communicating in real time means that if you send a message to another person who is online, that message appears on the person's computer right away. If that person sends you a response, it appears on your computer right away. In OS X Mountain Lion, you use the Messages application to exchange instant messages.

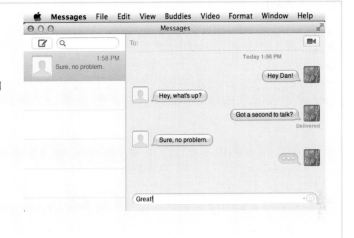

Share via Twitter

If you have an account on Twitter, you can configure OS X with your Twitter credentials. You can then share information with your Twitter followers by sending tweets from a number of OS X applications, including Safari and iPhoto. You can also use the Photo Booth application to take your picture, and then use that photo as your Twitter profile picture.

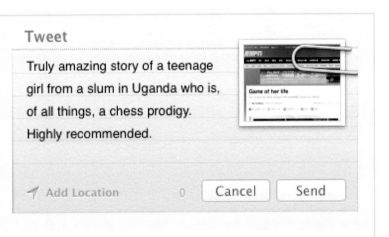

Place Video Calls

OS X Mountain Lion comes with a program called FaceTime that enables you to make video calls to other people. With a video call, your image is captured by a video camera — such as the iSight camera built into many Macs — and a microphone captures your voice. Both the video and audio streams are sent to the other person, who could be using FaceTime on a Mac, an iPhone 4 or later, or an iPad 2 or later. The other person can also see and hear you.

Organize Your Contacts and Appointments

You can use OS X to help you organize various aspects of your life. For example, OS X comes with tools that enable you to enter, edit, organize, and work with your contacts, which means you can maintain a convenient digital version of your address book. Other OS X tools enable you to schedule events such as appointments, meetings, and trips. You can even configure OS X to synchronize your contacts and schedule among multiple devices.

Maintain Your Contact List

OS X comes with an application called Contacts that enables you to store information about your contacts. For each contact, you can store data such as the person's name, address, telephone number, e-mail address, and birthday.

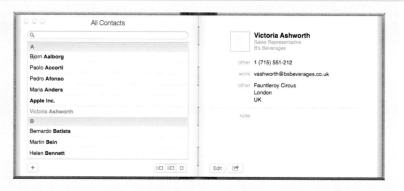

Work with Contacts

You can use your Contacts list to perform many different contact-related tasks. For example, you can use Mail to send a message either to individual contacts or to a contact group, which is a Contacts item that contains multiple contacts. Also, you can use Calendar to set up a meeting with one or more contacts.

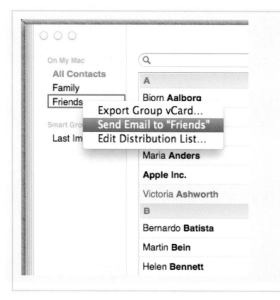

Schedule an Appointment

You can help organize your life by using OS X to record your appointments on the date and time they occur. You do this using the Calendar application, which uses an electronic calendar to store your appointments. You can even configure Calendar to display a reminder before an appointment occurs.

Schedule an All-Day Event

If an appointment has no set time — for example, a birthday, anniversary, or multiple-day event such as a sales meeting or vacation — you can use Calendar to set up the appointment as an all-day event.

Schedule a Repeating Appointment

If an appointment occurs regularly — for example, once a week or once every three months — you do not need to schedule every appointment manually. Instead, you can use Calendar to configure the activity as a repeating appointment, where you specify the repeat interval. Calendar then creates all the future appointments automatically.

Synchronize with iCloud

If you have an iCloud account, you can synchronize your OS X contacts and appointments so that they also appear in the iCloud Contacts and Calendar. If you have an iPod touch, iPhone, or iPad, you can use iCloud to sync those same contacts and appointments to your device. If you have a second Mac or a Windows PC, you can use iCloud to keep your contacts and appointments in sync on both computers.

Learning Basic OS X Program Tasks

One of the most crucial OS X concepts is the application (also sometimes called a program), because it is via applications that you perform all other OS X tasks. Therefore, it is important to have a basic understanding of how to start and manage applications in OS X. In this chapter, you take a tour of the OS X screen and the Dock, then you learn how to start an application, switch between running applications, and run applications full screen. You also learn how to control an application using pull-down menus, toolbars, and dialogs.

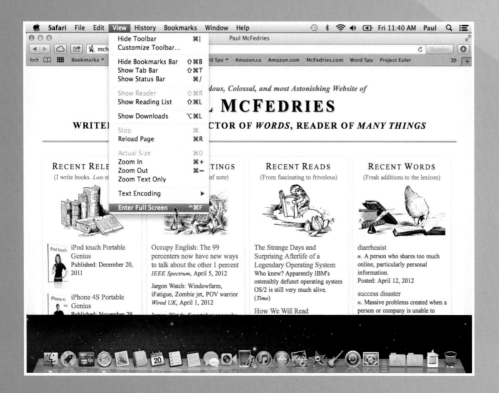

Explore the OS X Screen

Before you can begin to understand how the OS X operating system works, you should become familiar with the basic screen elements. These elements include the OS X menu bar, the desktop, desktop icons, and the Dock. Understanding where these elements appear on the screen and what they are used for will help you work through the rest of the tasks in this book and will help you navigate OS X and its applications on your own.

Ⓐ Menu Bar

The menu bar contains the pull-down menus for OS X and most Mac software.

Ⓑ Desktop

This is the OS X work area, where you work with your applications and documents.

Ⓒ Mouse Pointer

When you move your mouse or move your finger on a trackpad, the pointer moves along with it.

Ⓓ Desktop Icon

An icon on the desktop represents an application, a folder, a document, or a device attached to your Mac, such as a disk drive, a CD or DVD, or an iPod.

Ⓔ Dock

The Dock contains several icons, each of which gives you quick access to some commonly used applications.

Tour the Dock

The Dock is the strip that runs along the bottom of the Mac screen. The Dock is populated with several small images, which are called *icons*. Each icon represents a particular component of your Mac — an application, a folder, a document, and so on — and clicking the icon opens the component. This makes the Dock one of the most important and useful OS X features because it gives you one-click access to applications, folders, and documents. The icons shown here are typical, but your Mac may display a different arrangement.

A Finder
Work with the files on your computer.

B Launchpad
View, organize, and start your applications.

C Mission Control
Locate and navigate running applications.

D Safari
Browse the World Wide Web on the Internet.

E Mail
Send and receive e-mail messages.

F Contacts
Store and access people's names, addresses, and other contact information.

G Calendar
Record upcoming appointments, birthdays, meetings, and other events.

H Reminders
Set reminders for upcoming tasks.

I Notes
Record to-do lists and other short notes.

J Messages
Send instant messages to other people.

K FaceTime
Place video calls to other FaceTime users.

L Photo Booth
Take a picture using the camera on your Mac.

M iTunes
Play music and other media and add media to your iPod, iPhone, or iPad.

N App Store
Install new applications and upgrade existing ones.

O iPhoto
Import and edit digital photos and other images.

P iMovie
Import video footage and edit your own digital movies.

Q GarageBand
Create songs, podcasts, and other audio files.

R Time Machine
Create and access backups of your files.

S System Preferences
Customize and configure your Mac.

T Applications
Display the contents of your Applications folder.

U Documents
Display the contents of your Documents folder.

V Downloads
Display the contents of your Downloads folder.

W Trash
Delete files, folders, and applications.

Start an Application

To perform tasks of any kind in OS X, you use one of the applications installed on your Mac. The application you use depends on the task you want to perform. For example, if you want to surf the World Wide Web, you use a web browser application, such as the Safari program that comes with OS X. Before you can use an application, however, you must first tell OS X which application you want to run. OS X launches the application and displays it on the desktop. You can then use the application's tools to perform your tasks.

Start an Application

1 Click the **Finder** icon (□).

Note: *If the application that you want to start has an icon in the Dock, you can click the icon to start the application and skip the rest of these steps.*

The Finder window appears.

2 Click **Applications**.

Note: *You can also navigate to Applications in any Finder window by pressing* Shift *+* ⌘ *+* A *or by choosing Go and then clicking Applications.*

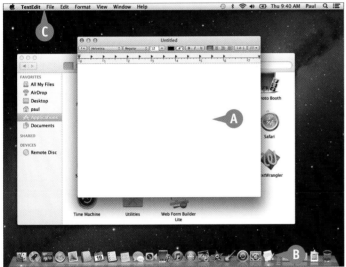

The Applications window appears.

3 Double-click the icon of the application that you want to start.

Note: *If you see a folder icon (▨), it means that the application resides in its own folder, which is a storage area on the computer. Double-click ▨ to open the folder and then double-click the application icon.*

A The application appears on the desktop.

B OS X adds a button for the application to the Dock.

C The menu bar displays the menus associated with the application.

Note: *Another common way to launch an application is to use Finder to locate a document you want to work with, and then double-click that document.*

---

simplify it

How do I add an icon to the Dock for an application I use frequently?
First, start the application as described in Steps **1** to **3**. Right-click the application's Dock icon, click Options, and then click **Keep in Dock**.

How do I shut down a running application?
The easiest way is to right-click the application's Dock icon and then click **Quit**. Alternatively, you can switch to the application and press ⌘+Q.

Start an Application Using Launchpad

You can start an application using the Launchpad feature. This is often faster than using the Applications folder, particularly for applications that do not have a Dock icon.

Launchpad is designed to mimic the Home screens of the iPhone, iPad, and iPhone touch. So if you own one or more of these devices, then you are already familiar with how Launchpad works.

Start an Application Using Launchpad

1 Click the **Launchpad** icon ([image]).

The Launchpad screen appears.

2 If the application you want to start resides in a different Launchpad screen, click the dot that corresponds to the screen.

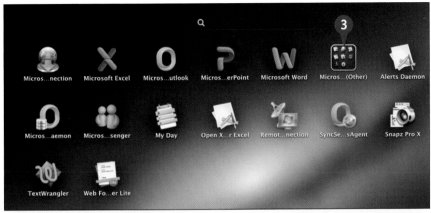

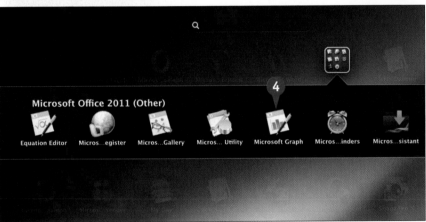

Launchpad switches to the screen and displays the applications.

③ If the application you want to start resides within a folder, click the folder.

Launchpad opens the folder.

④ Click the icon of the application you want to start.

OS X starts the application.

The dots that represent each Launchpad screen are quite small, making them hard to click with the mouse. Is there an easier way to navigate the Launchpad screens?
Yes. As mentioned earlier, OS X Mountain Lion has designed Launchpad to look somewhat similar to the Home screens of the iPhone, iPad, and iPhone touch. Another similarity is how you navigate the screens.

On an iPhone, iPad, and iPhone touch, you navigate the Home screens by using a finger to swipe the screen right or left. With your Mac, you can also navigate the Launchpad screens by swiping. In this case, however, you must use two fingers, and you swipe right or left on either the trackpad or the surface of a Magic Mouse.

Switch Between Applications

If you plan on running multiple applications at the same time, you need to know how to easily switch from one application to another. In OS X, after you start one application, you do not need to close that application before you open another one. OS X supports a feature called *multitasking*, which means running two or more applications at once. This is handy if you need to use several applications throughout the day. For example, you might keep your word processing application, your web browser, and your e-mail application open all day.

Switch Between Applications

1 Click the Dock icon of the application that you want to switch to.

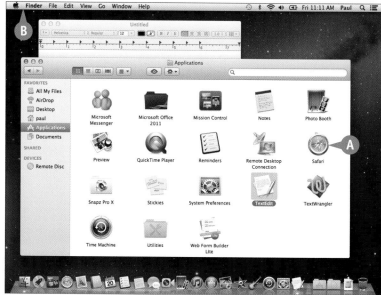

A OS X brings the application window(s) to the foreground.

B The menu bar displays the menus associated with the application.

Note: *To switch between applications from the keyboard, press and hold ⌘ and repeatedly press ⟨Tab⟩ until the application that you want is highlighted in the list of running applications. Release ⌘ to switch to the application.*

View Running Applications with Mission Control

The Mission Control feature, which was new in OS X Lion, makes it easier for you to navigate and locate your running applications. OS X allows you to open multiple applications at once, and the only real limit to the number of open applications you can have is the amount of memory contained in your Mac. In practical terms, this means you can easily open several applications, some of which may have multiple open windows. To help locate and navigate to the window you need, use the Mission Control feature.

View Running Applications with Mission Control

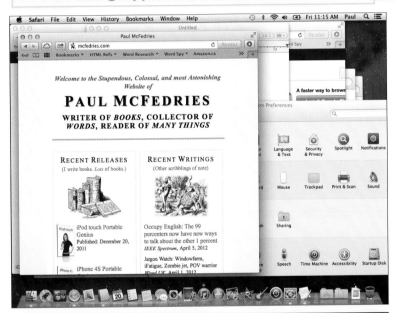

1 Place three fingers on the trackpad of your Mac and then swipe up.

Note: *You can also invoke Mission Control by pressing* F3.

Ⓐ Mission Control displays each open window.

Ⓑ Mission Control groups windows from the same application.

To switch to a particular window, click it.

Ⓒ To close Mission Control without selecting a window, click **Desktop** or press Esc.

Tour an Application Window

When you start an application, it appears on the OS X desktop in its own window. Each application has a unique window layout, but almost all application windows have a few features in common. To get the most out of your applications and to start working quickly and efficiently in an application, you need to know what these common features are and where to find them within the application window.

A Close Button

Click the **Close** button (⊙) to remove the application window from the desktop, usually without exiting the application.

B Minimize Button

Click the **Minimize** button (⊙) to remove the window from the desktop and display an icon for the currently open document in the right side of the Dock. The window is still open, but not active.

C Zoom Button

Click the **Zoom** button (⊙) to enlarge the window so that it can display all of its content, or as much of its content as can fit the screen.

D Toolbar

The toolbar contains buttons that offer easy access to common application commands and features, although not all applications have toolbars. To move the window, click and drag the toolbar.

E Status Bar

The status bar displays information about the current state of the application or document.

F Vertical Scroll Bar

Click and drag the vertical scroll bar to navigate up and down in a document.

G Horizontal Scroll Bar

Click and drag the horizontal scroll bar to navigate left and right in a document.

H Resize Control

Click and drag any edge or corner of the window to make the window larger or smaller.

Run an Application Full Screen

You can maximize the viewing and working areas of an application by running that application in full-screen mode. When you switch to full-screen mode, OS X hides the menu bar, the application's status bar, the Dock, and the top section of the application window (the section that includes the Close, Minimize, and Zoom icons). OS X then expands the rest of the application window so that it takes up the entire screen. You must be running OS X Lion or Mountain Lion to use full-screen mode. Note, too, that not all programs are capable of switching to full-screen mode.

Run an Application Full Screen

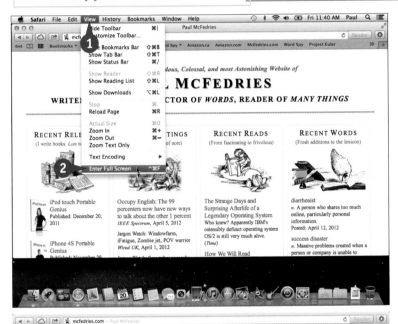

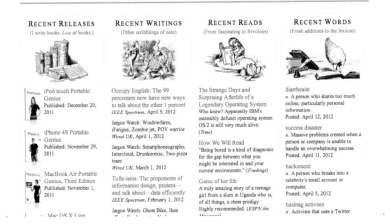

1 Click **View**.

2 Click **Enter Full Screen**.

You can also press `Control`+`⌘`+`F`.

You can also click **Full Screen** (▢).

OS X expands the application window to take up the entire screen.

Note: *To exit full-screen mode, move the mouse ▸ up to the top of the screen to reveal the menu bar, click* **View**, *and then click* **Exit Full Screen***. You can also press* `Control`+`⌘`+`F`*.*

Select a Command from a Pull-Down Menu

When you are working in an application, you can use the menu bar to access the application's commands and features. Each item in the menu bar represents a *pull-down menu*, a collection of commands usually related to each other in some way. For example, the

File menu commands usually deal with file-related tasks such as opening and closing documents. The items in a menu are either commands that execute an action in the application, or features that you can turn on and off.

Select a Command from a Pull-Down Menu

Execute Commands

1 Click the name of the menu that you want to display.

A The application displays the menu.

2 Click the command that you want to execute.

The application executes the command.

B If a command is followed by an ellipsis (...), it means the command displays a dialog.

C If a command is followed by an arrow (▶), it means the command displays a submenu. Click the command to open the submenu and then click the command that you want to run.

Turn Features On and Off

1 Click the name of the menu that you want to display.

D The application displays the menu.

2 Click the menu item. You may have to click for a submenu if your command is not on the main menu.

The application turns the feature either on or off.

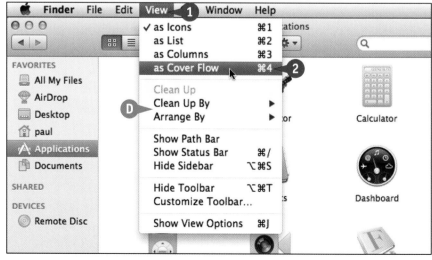

Select a Command Using a Toolbar

You can access many application commands faster by using the toolbar. Many applications come with a toolbar, which is a collection of buttons, lists, and other controls displayed in a strip, usually across the top of the application window. Because the toolbar is always visible, you can always use it to select commands, which means that the toolbar often gives you one-click access to the application's most common features. This is faster than using the menu bar method, which often takes several clicks, depending on the command.

Select a Command Using a Toolbar

Turn Features On and Off

1 Click the toolbar button that represents the feature you want to turn on.

A The application turns the feature on and indicates this state by highlighting the toolbar button.

B When a feature is turned off, the application does not highlight the button.

Execute Commands

1 Click the toolbar button that represents the command that you want.

2 If the button displays a menu, click the command on the menu.

C The application executes the command.

31

Select Options with Dialog Controls

You often interact with an application by selecting options or typing text using a dialog. A *dialog* is a small window that appears when an application has information for you, or needs you to provide information. For example, when you select the File menu's Print command to print a document, you use the Print dialog to specify the number of copies that you want to print.

You provide that and other information by accessing various types of dialog controls. To provide information to an application quickly and accurately, you need to know what these dialog controls look like and how they work.

A Command Button

Clicking a command button executes the command printed on the button face. For example, you can click **OK** to apply settings that you have chosen in a dialog, or you can click **Cancel** to close the dialog without changing the settings.

B Text Box

A text box enables you to enter typed text. Use the Del key to delete any existing characters, and then type your text.

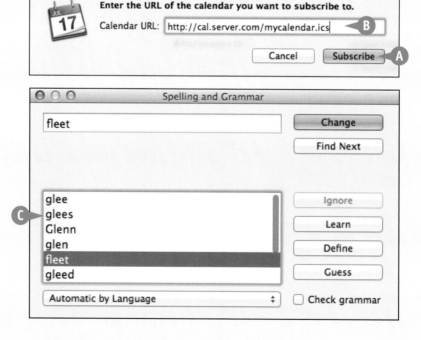

C List Box

A list box displays a list of choices from which you select the item you want. Use the vertical scroll bar to bring the item you want into view, and then click the item to select it.

Ⓓ Tabs

Many dialogs offer a large number of controls, so related controls appear on different tabs, and the tab names and icons appear across the top of the dialog. Click a tab to see its controls.

Ⓔ Pop-Up Menu

A pop-up menu displays a list of choices from which you select the item you want. Click the up-down arrows (▢) to pop up the menu, and then click the item that you want to select.

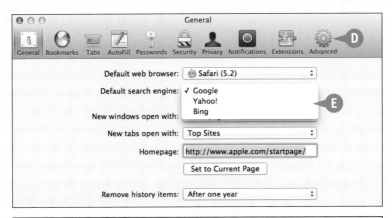

Ⓕ Check Box

Clicking a check box toggles an application feature on and off. If you are turning on a feature, the check box changes from ☐ to ☑; if you are turning off the feature, the check box changes from ☑ to ☐.

Ⓖ Radio Button

Clicking a radio button turns on an application feature. Only one radio button in a group can be turned on at a time. When you click a radio button that is currently off, it changes from ◯ to ⦿; a radio button that is on changes from ⦿ to ◯.

CHAPTER 3

Learning Basic OS X Document Tasks

Much of the work you do in OS X will involve documents, which are files that contain text, images, and other data. These tasks include saving, opening, printing, and editing documents, as well as copying and renaming files. To perform these and other tasks, it is important to have a basic understanding of how to work with and manage documents in OS X.

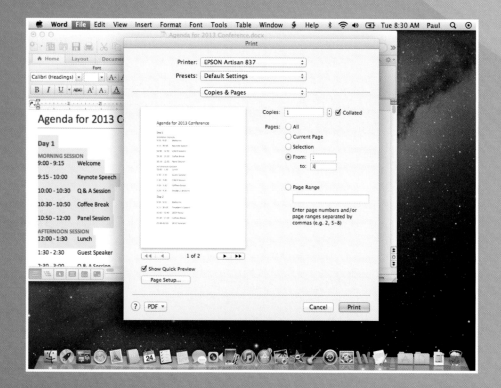

Save a Document

After you create a document and make changes to it, you can save the document to preserve your work. When you work on a document, OS X stores the changes in your computer's memory. However, OS X erases the contents of the Mac's memory each time you shut down or restart the computer. This means that the changes you have made to your document are lost when you turn off or restart your Mac. However, saving the document preserves your changes on your Mac's hard disk.

Save a Document

1 Click **File**.

2 Click **Save**.

In most applications, you can also press ⌘+S.

If you have saved the document previously, your changes are now preserved, and you do not need to follow the rest of the steps in this section.

If this is a new document that you have never saved before, the Save dialog appears.

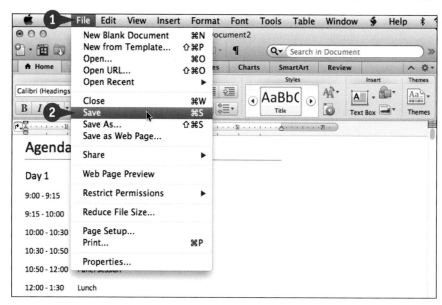

3 Type the filename you want to use in the Save As text box.

Ⓐ To store the file in a different folder, you can click the **Where** pop-up menu (⬍) and then select the location that you prefer.

4 Click **Save**.

The application saves the file.

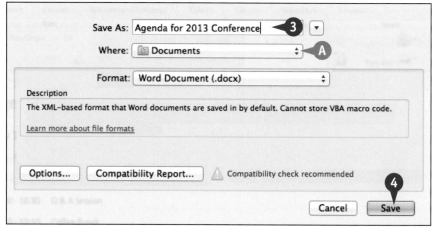

Open a Document

To work with a document that you have saved in the past, you can open it in the application that you used to create it. When you save a document, you save its contents to your Mac's hard disk, and those contents are stored in a separate file. When you open the document using the same application that you used to save it, OS X loads the file's contents into memory and displays the document in the application. You can then view or edit the document as needed.

Open a Document

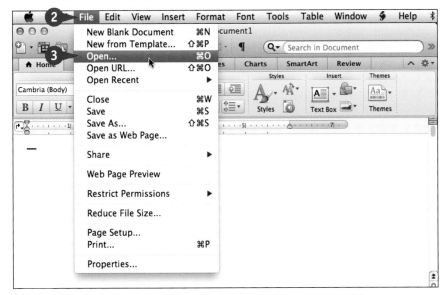

① Start the application that you want to work with.

② Click **File**.

③ Click **Open**.

In most applications, you can also press ⌘+O.

The Open dialog appears.

Ⓐ To select a different folder from which to open the file, you can click ⬦ and then click the location that you prefer.

④ Click the document.

⑤ Click **Open**.

The document appears in a window on the desktop.

Print a Document

When you need a hard copy of your document, either for your files or to distribute to someone else, you can send the document to your printer. Most applications that deal with documents also come with a Print command. When you run this command,

the Print dialog appears. You use the Print dialog to choose the printer you want to use, as well as to specify how many copies you want to print. Many Print dialogs also enable you to see a preview of your document before printing it.

Print a Document

1 Turn on your printer.

2 Open the document that you want to print.

3 Click **File**.

4 Click **Print**.

In many applications, you can select the Print command by pressing ⌘+P.

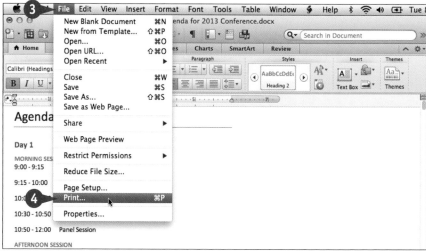

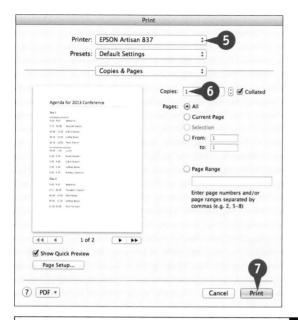

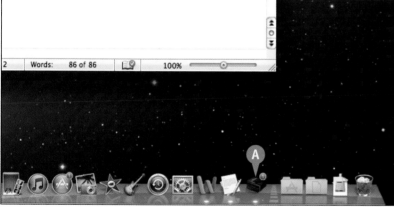

The Print dialog appears.

The layout of the Print dialog varies from application to application. The version shown here is a typical example.

5 If you have more than one printer, click ⬍ in the Printer list to select the printer that you want to use.

6 To print more than one copy, use the **Copies** text box to type the number of copies to print.

7 Click **Print**.

A OS X prints the document. The printer's icon appears in the Dock while the document prints.

---

simplify it

Can I print only part of my document?
In most applications, you can print a range of pages by selecting the **From** option (◯ changes to ◉) and then using the two text boxes to type the numbers of the first and last pages you want to print.

To print one page, click anywhere within the page before running the Print command; then select the **Current Page** option (◯ changes to ◉).

To print a section of the document, select the text before running the Print command, and then select the **Selection** option (◯ changes to ◉).

Pages: ◯ All
        ◯ Current Page
        ◯ Selection
        ◉ From: 1
            to: 3

Edit Document Text

When you work with a character-based file, such as a text or word processing document or an e-mail message, you need to know the basic techniques for editing, selecting, copying, and moving text. It is rare that any text you enter into a document is perfect the first time through. It is far more likely that the text contains errors that require correcting, or words, sentences, or paragraphs that appear in the wrong place. To get your document text the way you want it, you need to know how to edit text, including deleting characters, selecting the text you want to work with, and copying and moving text.

Edit Document Text

Delete Characters

1 In a text document, click immediately to the right of the last character that you want to delete.

A The cursor appears after the character.

Agenda for 2013 Conference

Day 1

MORNING SESSION
9:00 - 9:15	Welcome
9:15 - 10:00	Keynote Speech
10:00 - 10:30	Q & A Session
10:30 - 10:50	Coffee Break
10:50 - 12:00	Panel Session
12:00 - 1:30	Lunch

AFTERNOON SESSION
1:30 - 2:30	Guest Speaker
2:30 - 3:00	Q & A Session
3:00 - 3:20	Coffeee Break
3:20 - 4:00	A Look at the Future of the Industry
4:00 - 5:00	Breakout Sessions

2 Press **Del** until you have deleted all the characters you want.

If you make a mistake, immediately click **Edit**, and then click **Undo**. You can also press ⌘+Z.

Agenda for 2013 Conference

Day 1

MORNING SESSION
9:00 - 9:15	Welcome
9:15 - 10:00	Keynote Speech
10:00 - 10:30	Q & A Session
10:30 - 10:50	Coffee Break
10:50 - 12:00	Panel Session
12:00 - 1:30	Lunch

AFTERNOON SESSION
1:30 - 2:30	Guest Speaker
2:30 - 3:00	Q & A Session
3:00 - 3:20	Coffeee Break
3:20 - 4:00	A Look at the Future
4:00 - 5:00	Breakout Sessions

Agenda for 2013 Conference

Day 1

MORNING SESSION 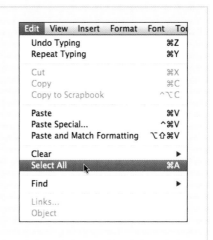❶

9:00 - 9:15	Welcome
9:15 - 10:00	Keynote Speech
10:00 - 10:30	Q & A Session
10:30 - 10:50	Coffee Break
10:50 - 12:00	Panel Session
12:00 - 1:30	Lunch

AFTERNOON SESSION

Agenda for 2013 Conference

❷ **Day 1**

MORNING SESSION ◀ Ⓑ

9:00 - 9:15	Welcome
9:15 - 10:00	Keynote Speech
10:00 - 10:30	Q & A Session
10:30 - 10:50	Coffee Break
10:50 - 12:00	Panel Session
12:00 - 1:30	Lunch

AFTERNOON SESSION

Select Text for Editing

❶ Click and drag across the text that you want to select.

❷ Release the mouse button.

Ⓑ The application highlights the selected text.

simplify it

Are there any shortcut methods for selecting text?
Yes, most OS X applications have shortcuts you can use. Here are the most useful ones:

- Double-click a word to select it.
- Hold down **Shift** and press ➡ or ⬅ to select entire words.
- Hold down **Shift** and ⌘ and press ➡ to select to the end of the line, or ⬅ to select to the beginning of the line.
- Triple-click inside a paragraph to select it.
- Click **Edit** and then click **Select All**, or press ⌘+A to select the entire document.

Edit	View	Insert	Format	Font	To
Undo Typing					⌘Z
Repeat Typing					⌘Y
Cut					⌘X
Copy					⌘C
Copy to Scrapbook					⌃⌥C
Paste					⌘V
Paste Special...					⌃⌘V
Paste and Match Formatting					⌥⇧⌘V
Clear					▶
Select All					⌘A
Find					▶
Links...					
Object					

continued

Edit Document
Text *(continued)*

Once you select text, you can then copy or move the text to another location in your document. Copying text is often a useful way to save work. For example, if you want to use the same passage of text elsewhere in the document, you can copy it instead of typing it from scratch. If you need a similar passage in another part of the document, copy the original and then edit the copy as needed. If you entered a passage of text in the wrong position within the document, you can fix that by moving the text to the correct location.

Edit Document Text *(continued)*

Copy Text

1 Select the text that you want to copy.

2 Click **Edit**.

3 Click **Copy**.

In most applications, you can also press ⌘+C.

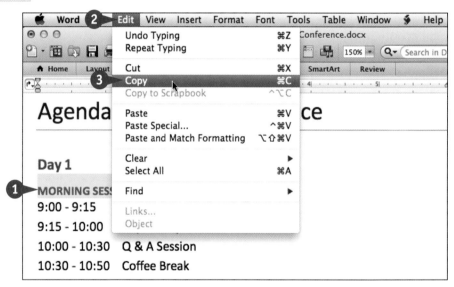

4 Click inside the document where you want the copied text to appear.

The cursor appears in the position where you clicked.

5 Click **Edit**.

6 Click **Paste**.

In most applications, you can also press ⌘+V.

Ⓐ The application inserts a copy of the selected text at the cursor position.

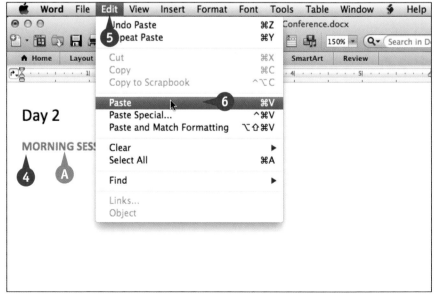

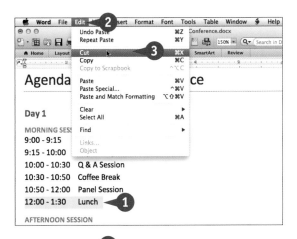

Move Text

1 Select the text that you want to move.

2 Click **Edit**.

3 Click **Cut**.

In most applications, you can also press ⌘+X.

The application removes the text from the document.

4 Click inside the document where you want to move the text.

The cursor appears at the position where you clicked.

5 Click **Edit**.

6 Click **Paste**.

In most applications, you can also press ⌘+V.

B The application inserts the text at the cursor position.

How do I move and copy text with my mouse?

First, select the text that you want to move or copy. To move the selected text, position the mouse pointer over the selection and then click and drag the text to the new position within the document.

To copy the selected text, position the mouse pointer over the selection, press and hold the Option key, and then click and drag the text (the mouse ▶ changes to ▶) to the new position within the document.

Copy a File

You can use OS X to make an exact copy of a file. This is useful when you want to make an extra copy of an important file to use as a backup. Similarly, you might require a copy of a file if you want to send the copy on a disk to another person. Finally, copying a file is also a real timesaver if you need a new file very similar to an existing file: You copy the original file and then make the required changes to the copy. You can copy either a single file or multiple files. You can also use this technique to copy a folder.

Copy a File

1 Locate the file that you want to copy.

2 Open the folder to which you want to copy the file.

To open a second folder window, click **File** and then click **New Finder Window**, or press ⌘+N.

3 Press and hold the Option key, and then click and drag the file and drop it inside the destination folder.

A The original file remains in its folder.

B A copy of the original file appears in the destination folder.

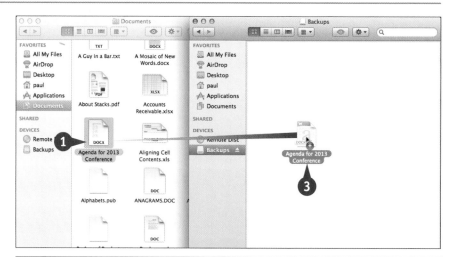

You can also make a copy of a file in the same folder, which is useful if you want to make major changes to the file and you would like to preserve a copy of the original. Click the file, click **File**, and then click **Duplicate**, or press ⌘+D. OS X creates a copy with the word "copy" added to the filename.

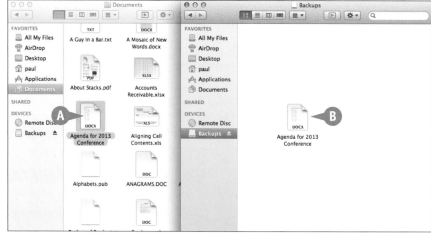

44

Move
a File

When you need to store a file in a new location, the easiest way is to move the file from its current folder to another folder on your Mac. When you save a file for the first time, you specify a folder on your Mac's hard disk. This original location is not permanent,

however. Using the technique in this section, you can move the file to another location on your Mac's hard disk. You can use this technique to move a single file, multiple files, and even a folder.

Move a File

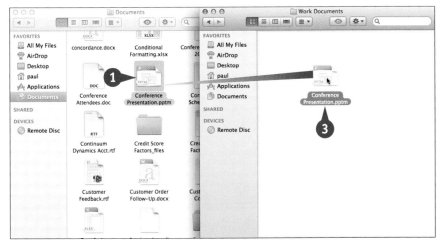

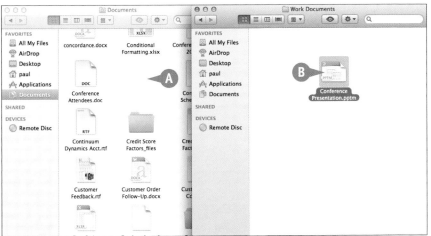

1 Locate the file that you want to move.

2 Open the folder to which you want to move the file.

To create a new destination folder in the current folder, click **File** and then click **New Folder**, or press Shift+⌘+N.

3 Click and drag the file and drop it inside the destination folder.

Note: *If you are moving the file to another disk drive, you must hold down ⌘ while you click and drag the file.*

Ⓐ The file disappears from its original folder.

Ⓑ The file moves to the destination folder.

Rename a File

You can change the name of a file, which is useful if the current filename does not accurately describe the contents of the file. By giving your document a descriptive name, you make it easier to find the file later. You should rename only those documents that you have created or that have been given to you by someone else. Do not try to rename any of the OS X system files or any files associated with your applications, or your computer may behave erratically, or even crash.

Rename a File

① Open the folder containing the file that you want to rename.

② Click the file.

③ Press Return.

Ⓐ A text box appears around the filename.

You can also rename any folders that you have created.

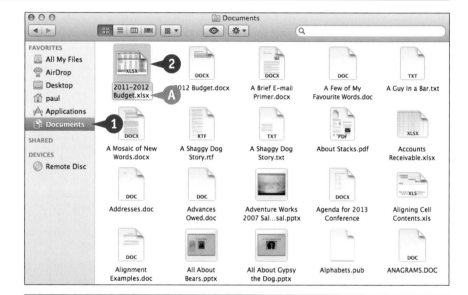

④ Edit the existing name or type a new name that you want to use for the file.

If you decide that you do not want to rename the file after all, you can press Esc to cancel the operation.

⑤ Press Return or click an empty section of the folder.

Ⓑ The new name appears under the file icon.

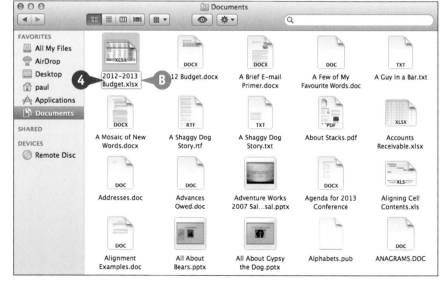

Delete a File

When you no longer need a file, you can delete it. This helps to prevent your hard drive from becoming cluttered with unnecessary files. You should ensure that you delete only those documents that you have created or that have been given to you by someone else. Do not delete any of the OS X system files or any files associated with your applications, or your computer may behave erratically, or even crash.

Delete a File

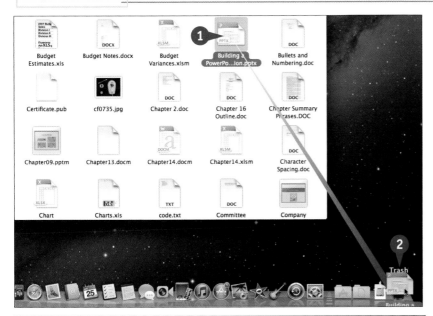

① Locate the file that you want to delete.

② Click and drag the file and drop it on the Trash icon in the Dock.

Ⓐ The file disappears from the folder.

You can also delete a file by clicking it and then pressing ⌘+Del.

If you delete a file accidentally, you can restore it. Simply click the Dock's Trash icon to open the Trash window. Click and drag the file from the Trash window and drop it back in its original folder.

CHAPTER 4

Browsing the World Wide Web

The *World Wide Web*, or simply, the web, is a massive storehouse of information that resides on computers, called *web servers*, located all over the world. Information is presented on *web pages* that you download to your computer using a web browser program, such as the OS X Safari application. Each web page can combine text with images, sounds, music, and even videos to present information on a particular subject. The web consists of billions of pages covering almost every imaginable topic. A *website* is a collection of web pages associated with a particular person or organization. If your Mac is connected to the Internet, you can use the Safari browser to navigate, or *surf*, websites.

Open and Close Safari

In OS X, the default web browser is Safari, which you can use to surf websites when your Mac is connected to the Internet.

The Safari application offers a number of features that make it easier to browse the web. For example, you can open multiple pages in a single Safari window, and you can save your favorite sites for easier access.

To use these features, you must know how to start the Safari application. When you have finished surfing the web, you need to know how to shut down Safari to save system resources on your Mac.

Open and Close Safari

Open Safari

1 In the Dock, click the **Safari** icon (⊚).

The Safari window appears.

Note: *The initial web page you see depends on how your version of Safari has been configured. In most cases, you see the Apple.com Start page.*

Close Safari

1 Click **Safari**.

2 Click **Quit Safari**.

Are there other methods I can use to open Safari?
If you have removed the 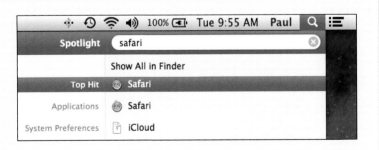 icon from the Dock, there are a couple of other quick methods you can use to start Safari. If you have used Safari recently, click 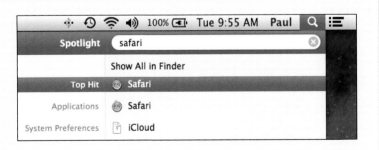, click **Recent Items**, and then click **Safari**. You can also click Spotlight (🔍), type **safari**, and then click **Safari** in the search results.

Select a Link

Almost all web pages include links to other pages that contain related information. Web page links come in two forms: text and images. Text links consist of a word or phrase that usually appears underlined and in a different color from the rest of the page text. However, web page designers can control the look of their links, so text links may not always stand out in this way.

The only way to tell for sure is to position the mouse pointer (↖) over the text or image; if the ↖ changes to ✋, you know the item is a link.

Select a Link

1 Position the mouse ↖ over the link (↖ changes to ✋).

2 Click the text or image.

A The status bar shows the address of the linked page.

Note: *The address shown in the status bar when you point at a link may be different from the one shown when the page is downloading. This occurs when the website "redirects" the link.*

Note: *If you do not see the status bar, click* **View** *and then click* **Show Status Bar**.

The linked web page appears.

B The web page title and address change after the linked page is loaded.

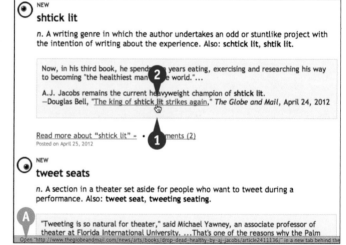

Enter a Web Page Address

If you know the address of a web page, you can type it into the browser to display the page. Every page is uniquely identified by an address called the Uniform Resource Locator, or URL (pronounced *yoo-ar-ell*).

The URL has four basic parts: the *transfer method* (usually HTTP, which stands for Hypertext Transfer Protocol), the website *domain name*, the *directory*

where the web page is located on the server, and the *web page filename*.

The website domain name suffix most often used is .com (commercial), but other common suffixes include .org (nonprofit organization), and country domains such as .ca (Canada).

Enter a Web Page Address

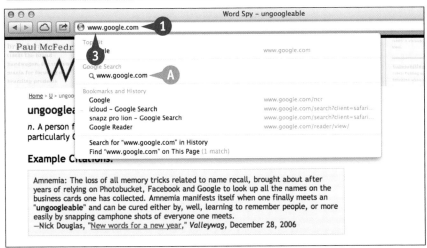

① Click inside the address bar.

② Press **Del** to delete the existing address.

③ Type the address of the web page you want to visit.

④ Press **Return**.

Ⓐ You can also click the site if it appears in the list of suggested sites.

The web page appears.

Ⓑ The web page title changes after the page is loaded.

Open a Web Page in a Tab

You can make it easier to work with multiple web pages and sites simultaneously by opening each page in its own tab. As you surf the web, you may come upon a page that you want to keep available while you visit other sites. Instead of leaving the page and

trying to find it again when you need it, Safari lets you leave the page open in a special section of the browser window called a *tab*. You can then use a second tab to visit your other sites, and to resume viewing the first site, you need only click its tab.

Open a Web Page in a Tab

Open a Link in a New Tab

1 Right-click the link you want to open.

2 Click **Open Link in New Tab**.

A A new tab appears with the page title.

3 Click the tab to display the page.

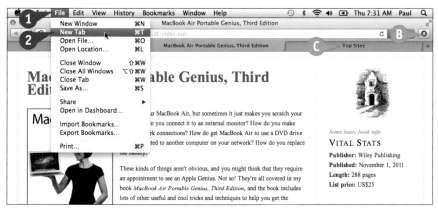

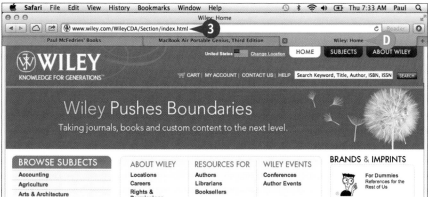

Create a New Tab

1 Click **File**.

2 Click **New Tab**.

B If you already have two or more tabs open, you can also click the **Create a new tab** icon (⊞).

C Safari creates a new tab.

3 Type the address of the page you want to load into the new tab.

4 Press Return.

D Safari displays the page in the tab.

Are there any shortcuts I can use to open web pages in tabs?
Yes, here are a few useful techniques:

● Press and hold ⌘ and click a link to open the page in a tab.

● Press and hold ⌘+Shift and click a link to open the page in a tab and display the tab.

● Type an address and then press ⌘+Return to open the page in a new tab.

● Type an address and then press Shift+⌘+Return to open the page in a new foreground tab.

● Press Shift+⌘+] or Shift+⌘+[to cycle through the tabs.

● Press ⌘+W to close the current tab.

● Press Option and click ⊗ to close every tab but the one you clicked.

Navigate
Web Pages

After you have visited several pages, you can return to a page you visited earlier. Instead of retyping the address or looking for the link, Safari gives you some easier methods. When you navigate from page to page, you create a kind of "path" through the web. Safari keeps track of this path by maintaining a list

of the pages you have visited. You can use that list to go back to a page you have visited. After you have gone back to a page you have visited, you can also use the same list of pages to go forward through the pages again.

Navigate Web Pages

Go Back One Page

1 Click the **Previous Page** icon (◄).

The previous page you visited appears.

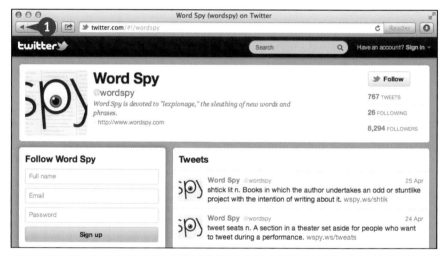

Go Back Several Pages

1 Click and hold down the mouse ▶ on ◄.

Note: *The list of visited pages is different for each tab that you have open. If you do not see the page you want, you may need to click a different tab.*

A list of the pages you have visited appears.

2 Click the page you want to revisit.

The page appears.

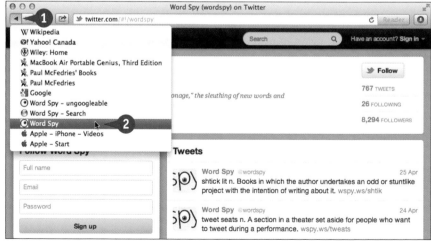

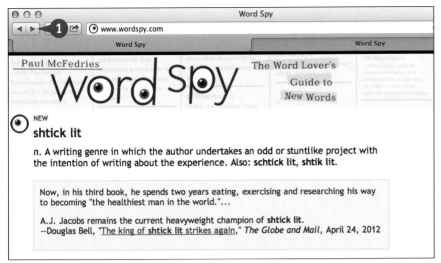

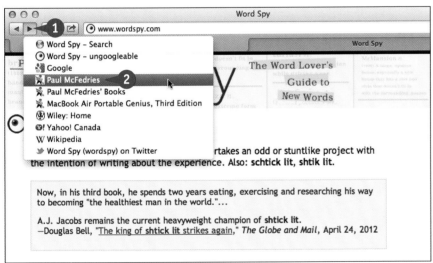

Go Forward One Page

1 Click the **Next Page** icon ().

The next page appears.

Note: *If you are at the last page viewed up to that point, ▶ is not active.*

Go Forward Several Pages

1 Click and hold down the mouse ▸ on ▶.

A list of the pages you have visited appears.

Note: *The list of visited pages is different for each tab that you have open. If you do not see the page you want, you may need to click a different tab.*

2 Click the page you want to revisit.

The page appears.

---

simplify it

Are there any shortcuts I can use to navigate web pages?
Yes, a few useful keyboard shortcuts you can use are

● Press ⌘+[to go back one page.

● Press ⌘+] to go forward one page.

● Press Shift+⌘+H to return to the Safari home page (the first page you see when you open Safari).

Navigate with the History List

The Previous Page and Next Page buttons (◄ and ►) enable you to navigate pages in the current browser session. To redisplay sites that you have visited in the past few days or weeks, you need to use the History list, which is a collection of the websites and pages you have visited over the past month.

If you visit sensitive places such as an Internet banking site or your corporate site, you can increase security by clearing the history list so that other people cannot see where you have been.

Navigate with the History List

Load a Page from the History List

① Click **History**.

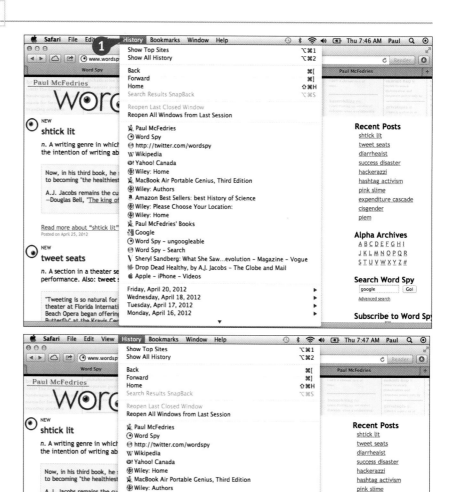

② Click the date when you visited the page.

A submenu of pages that you visited during that day appears.

③ Click the page you want to revisit.

Ⓐ The page appears.

Clear the History List

① Click **History**.

② Click **Clear History**.

Safari deletes all the pages from the history list.

Can I control the length of time that Safari keeps track of the pages I visit?
Yes, by following these steps:

① In the menu bar, click **Safari**.

② Click **Preferences**.

③ Click **General**.

④ In the Remove history items pop-up menu, click ⬚ and then click the amount of time you want Safari to track your history.

⑤ Click ⬜.

Change Your Home Page

Your home page is the web page that appears when you first start Safari. The default home page is the Apple.com Start page, but you can change that to any other page, or even to an empty page. This is useful if you do not use the Apple.com Start page, or if there is another page that you always visit at the start of your browsing session. For example, if you have your own website, it might make sense to begin there. Safari also has a command that enables you to view the home page at any time during your browsing session.

Change Your Home Page

Change the Home Page

1. Display the web page that you want to use as your home page.

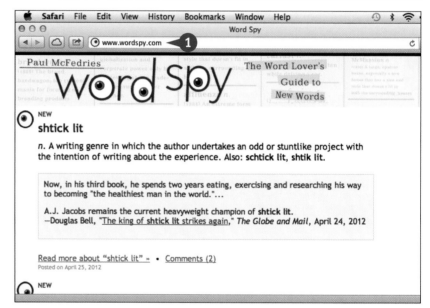

2. Click **Safari**.

3. Click **Preferences**.

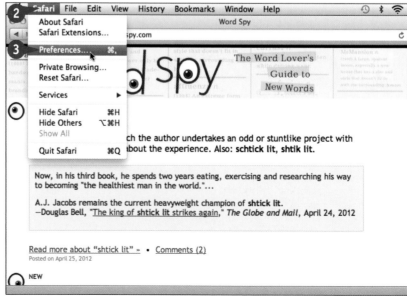

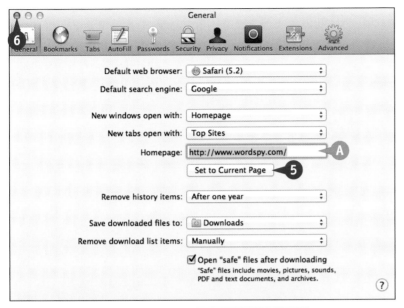

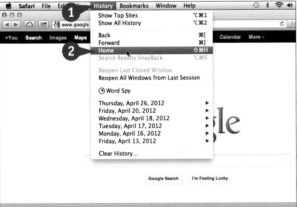

4 Click **General**.

5 Click **Set to Current Page**.

A Safari inserts the address of the current page in the Homepage text box.

Note: *If your Mac is not currently connected to the Internet, you can also type the new home page address manually using the Homepage text box.*

6 Click ⊙.

View the Home Page

1 Click **History**.

2 Click **Home**.

Note: *You can also display the home page by pressing* Shift + ⌘ + H .

Safari displays the home page.

simplify it

Can I get Safari to open a new window without displaying the home page?
Yes, by following these steps:

1 In the menu bar, click **Safari**.

2 Click **Preferences**.

3 Click **General**.

4 In the New windows open with pop-up menu, click ⋮ and then click **Empty Page**.

5 Click ⊙.

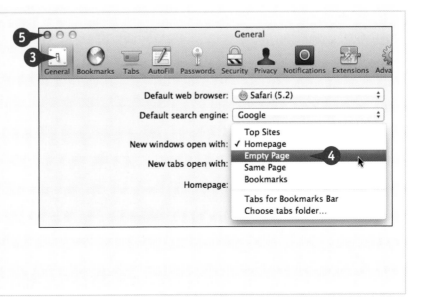

Bookmark Web Pages

If you have web pages that you visit frequently, you can save yourself time by storing those pages as bookmarks within Safari. This enables you to display the pages with just a couple of mouse clicks.

The bookmark stores the name as well as the address of the page. Most bookmarks are stored on the Safari Bookmarks menu. However, Safari also offers the Bookmarks bar, which appears just below the address bar. You can put your favorite sites on the Bookmarks bar for easiest access.

Bookmark Web Pages

Bookmark a Web Page

1 Display the web page you want to save as a bookmark.

2 Click **Bookmarks**.

3 Click **Add Bookmark**.

A You can also run the Add Bookmark command by clicking **Share** (⬆️) and then clicking **Add Bookmark**.

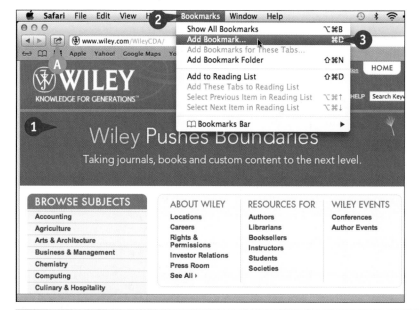

The Add Bookmark dialog appears.

Note: *You can also display the Add Bookmark dialog by pressing* ⌘+D.

4 Click 🔽 and then click the location where you want to store the bookmark.

5 Edit the page name, if necessary.

6 Click **Add**.

Safari adds a bookmark for the page.

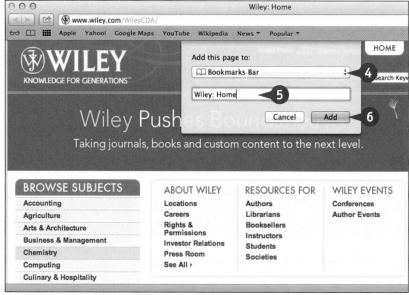

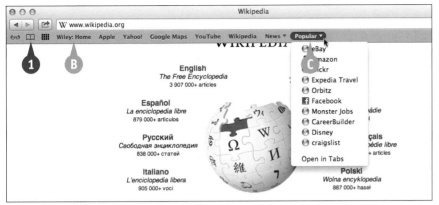

Display a Bookmarked Web Page

1 Click the **Show all bookmarks** button (📖).

B If you added the bookmark to the Bookmarks bar, click the page name.

C If you added the bookmark to a folder, click the folder and then click the page name.

The Bookmarks window appears.

2 Click ▶ to open the folder that contains the bookmark you want (▶ changes to ▼).

3 Double-click the bookmark.

The web page appears.

I use my Bookmarks bar a lot. Is there an easier way to display these pages?
Yes. Safari automatically assigns keyboard shortcuts to the first nine bookmarks, counting from left to right and not including folders. For example, you display the left-most bookmark by pressing ⌘+1. Moving to the right, the shortcuts are ⌘+2, ⌘+3, and so on.

How do I delete a bookmark?
On the Bookmarks bar, right-click the bookmark and then click **Delete**, or hold down ⌘ and drag it off the bar. For all other bookmarks, click 📖 to display the Bookmarks window. Locate the bookmark you want to remove, right-click the bookmark, and then click **Delete**.

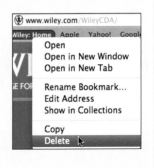

Search
for Sites

If you need information on a specific topic, Safari has a built-in feature that enables you to quickly search the web for sites that have the information you require. The web has a number of sites called **search engines** that enable you to find what you are looking for. By default, Safari uses the Google search site

(www.google.com). Simple, one-word searches often return tens of thousands of **hits**, or matching sites. To improve your searching, type multiple search terms that define what you are looking for. To search for a phrase, enclose the words in quotation marks.

Search for Sites

1 Click in the Address box.

2 Press Delete to delete the address.

3 Type a word, phrase, or question that represents the information you want to find.

A If you see the search text you want to use in the list of suggested searches, click the text and skip Step **4**.

4 Press Return.

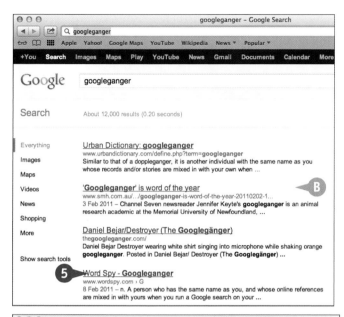

B A list of pages that match your search text appears.

5 Click a web page.

The page appears.

Is there an easy way that I can rerun a recent search?
Yes, Safari remembers your most recent search. Follow these steps to quickly rerun that search:

1 Click **History**.

2 Click **Search Results Snapback**.

You can also press Option + ⌘ + S.

Safari sends the search text to Google again.

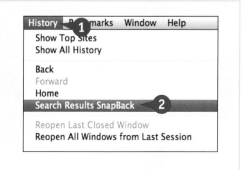

Download
a File

Some websites make files available for you to save to your Mac using Safari. Saving data from the Internet to your computer is called ***downloading***.

For certain types of files, Safari may display the content right away instead of letting you download it. This happens for files such as text documents and PDF files. In any case, to use a file from a website, you must have an application designed to work with that particular file type. For example, if the file is an Excel workbook, you need either Excel for the Mac or a compatible program.

Download a File

1 Navigate to the page that contains the link to the file.

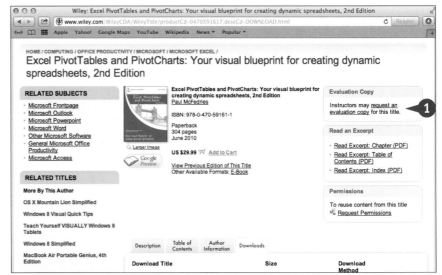

2 Click the link to the file.

Safari downloads the file to your Mac.

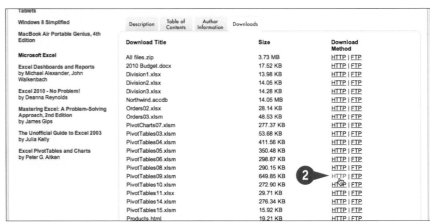

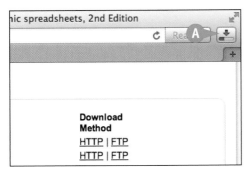

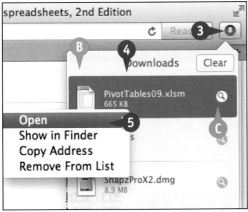

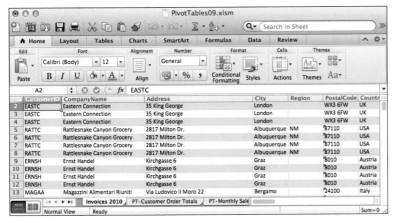

A The Show Downloads button shows the progress of the download.

3 When the download is complete, click the Show Downloads button ().

4 Right-click the file.

B You can also double-click the icon to the left of the file.

C If you want to access the downloaded file, click **Show in Finder** ( ) to view the file in the Downloads folder.

5 Click **Open**.

The file opens in the corresponding application.

simplify it

If Safari displays the file instead of downloading it, how do I save the file to my Mac?
Click **File** and then click **Save As**. Type a name for the new file, choose a folder, and then click **Save**.

Is it safe to download files from the web?
Yes, as long as you only download files from sites you trust. If you ever notice that Safari is attempting to download a file without your permission, cancel the download immediately because it is likely the file contains a virus or other malware. If you do not completely trust a file you have downloaded, use an antivirus program — such as ClamXav; see www.clamxav.com — to scan the file before you open it.

CHAPTER 5

Communicating via E-mail

OS X comes with the Apple Mail application that you can use to exchange e-mail messages. After you enter your account details into Mail, you can send e-mail to friends, family, colleagues, and even total strangers almost anywhere in the world. You can also attach documents, images, and other types of files to your e-mail messages. With Mail, you can also read the messages that people send to you, reply to those messages, and forward those messages to other people.

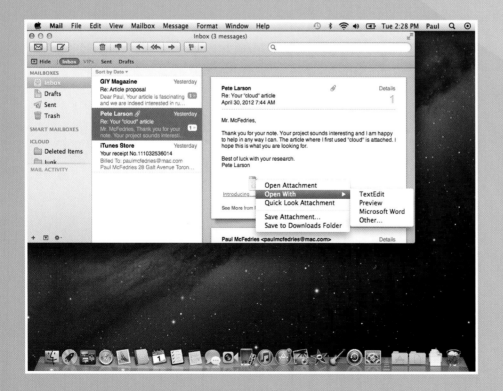

Open and Close Mail

You use the Mail application to exchange and manage e-mail messages. E-mail is one of the most popular Internet services because it offers three main advantages: It is universal, fast, and convenient.

E-mail is universal because nearly anyone who can access the Internet has an e-mail address. E-mail is fast because messages are generally delivered within a few minutes. E-mail is convenient because you can send messages at any time of day, and your recipient does not need to be at the computer or connected to the Internet. Before you can use e-mail, you must know how to start the Mail application.

Open and Close Mail

Open Mail

1 In the Dock, click the **Mail** icon (■).

Note: *If the Welcome to Mail dialog appears, see the next section to learn how to set up your first e-mail account in Mail.*

The Mail window appears.

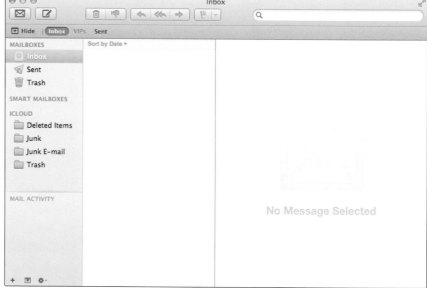

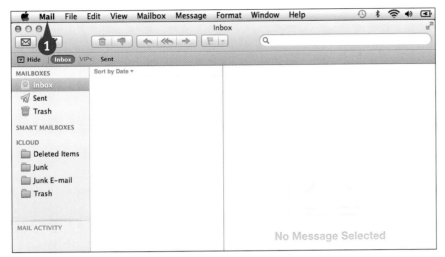

Close Mail

1 Click **Mail**.

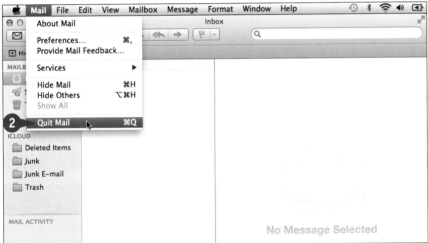

2 Click **Quit Mail**.

simplify it

Are there other methods I can use to open Mail?

If you have removed the 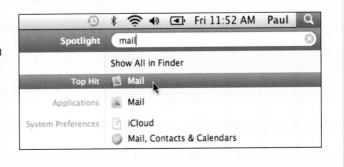 icon from the Dock, there are a couple of other quick methods you can use to start Mail. If you have used Mail recently, click ![apple], click **Recent Items**, and then click **Safari**. You can also click **Spotlight** (![search]), type **Mail**, and then click **Mail** in the search results.

Add an E-mail Account

Before you can send and receive e-mail messages, you must add your e-mail account to the Mail application. Your e-mail account is usually a POP (Post Office Protocol) account supplied by your Internet service provider, which should have supplied you with the account details. You can also set up

web-based e-mail accounts with services such as Hotmail and Gmail. A web-based account is convenient because it enables you to send and receive messages from any computer. If you have an Apple ID, you can also set up Mail with your Apple account details.

Add an E-mail Account

Get Started Adding an Account

1 Click **File**.

2 Click **Add Account**.

Note: *If you are just starting Mail and the Welcome to Mail dialog is on-screen, you can skip Steps 1 and 2.*

The Add Account dialog appears. If you are starting Mail for the first time, the Welcome to Mail dialog is identical.

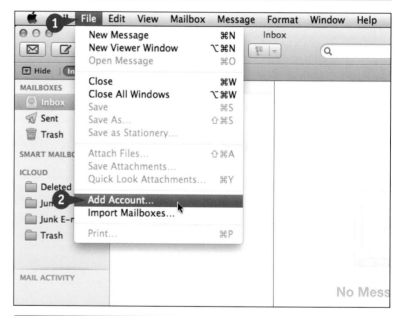

Add an Apple Account

1 Type your name.

2 Type your Apple account address.

3 Type your Apple account password.

4 Click **Create**.

Mail checks your Apple account.

5 Click **Create** (not shown).

Mail adds your Apple account.

Add a POP Account

1 Type your name.

2 Type your POP account address.

3 Type your POP account password and click **Continue**.

4 Click the **Account Type** pop-up menu (▯) and then click POP.

5 Type a description of the account.

6 Type the address of the account's incoming mail server.

7 Edit the User Name text as required and click **Continue**.

8 Type a description of the outgoing mail server.

9 Type the address of the outgoing mail server, which is sometimes called the SMTP server.

Ⓐ If your ISP requires authentication, click **Use Authentication** (☐ changes to ☑).

10 Click **Continue** (not shown).

11 Click **Create** (not shown).

---

simplify it

My e-mail account requires me to use a nonstandard outgoing mail port. How do I set this up?

1 In the menu bar, click **Mail**.

2 Click **Preferences**.

3 Click **Accounts**.

4 In the Outgoing Mail Server (SMTP) list, click ▯ and then click **Edit SMTP Server List**.

5 Click the outgoing mail server.

6 Click **Advanced**.

7 Click **Use custom port** (☐ changes to ◉).

8 Type the nonstandard port number.

9 Click **OK**.

10 Click ◯.

11 Click **Save**.

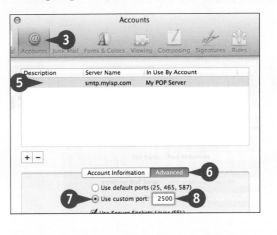

Send an E-mail Message

You can send an e-mail message to a person or organization if you know the address. An e-mail address is a set of characters that uniquely identifies the location of an Internet mailbox. Each address takes the form ***username@domain***, where ***username*** is the name of the person's account with the ISP or within his or her organization; and ***domain*** is the

Internet name of the company that provides the e-mail account. When you send an e-mail message, it travels through your ISP's outgoing mail server. This server routes the message to the recipient's incoming mail server, which then stores the message in the recipient's mailbox.

Send an E-mail Message

1 Click **New Message** (⬚).

> **Note:** *You can also start a new message by pressing* ⌘+N.

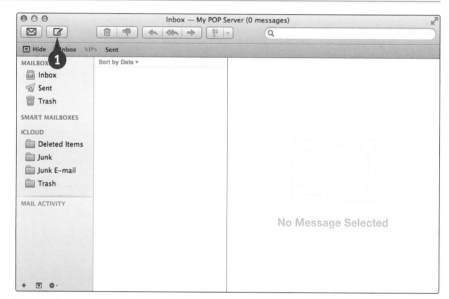

A message window appears.

2 Type the e-mail address of the person to whom you are sending the message in the To field box.

3 Type the e-mail address of the person to whom you are sending a copy of the message in the Cc field.

> **Note:** *You can add multiple e-mail addresses in both the To line and the Cc line b separating each address with a comma (,).*

4 Type a brief description of the message in the Subject field.

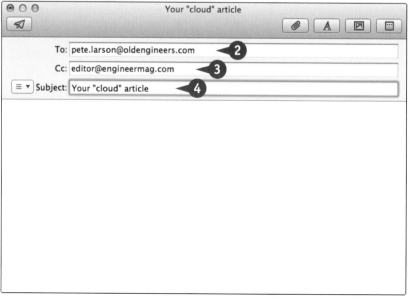

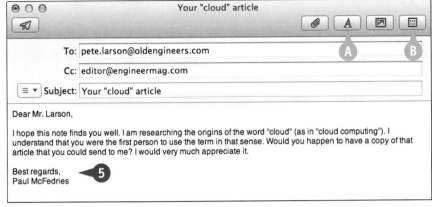

5 Type the message.

A To change the message font, click **Fonts** (A) to display the Font panel.

B To change the overall look of the message, click **Show Stationery** (□) and then click a theme.

Note: *Many people use e-mail programs that cannot process text formatting. Unless you are sure your recipient's program supports formatting, it is best to send plain-text messages. To do this, click* **Format** *and then click* **Make Plain Text**.

6 Click **Send** (✈).

Mail sends your message.

Note: *Mail stores a copy of your message in the Sent folder.*

simplify it

I have a large number of messages to compose. Do I have to be online to do this?
No, you can compose all the messages while you are offline. Follow these steps:

1 While disconnected from the Internet, start Mail.

2 To ensure you are working offline, click **Mailbox**. If the Take All Accounts Offline command is enabled, click that command.

3 Compose and send the message. Each time you click **Send** (✈), your message is stored temporarily in the Outbox folder.

4 When you are done, connect to the Internet.

After a few moments, Mail automatically sends all the messages in the Outbox folder.

Add a File Attachment

To send a document to another person, you can attach the document to an e-mail message. A typical e-mail message is fine for short notes, but you may have something more complex to communicate, such as budget numbers or a slide show, or some form of media that you want to share, such as an image or a song.

Because these more complex types of data usually come in a separate file — such as a spreadsheet, presentation file, or picture file — it makes sense to send that file to your recipient. You do this by attaching the file to an e-mail message.

Add a File Attachment

1 Click **New Message** (⧉).

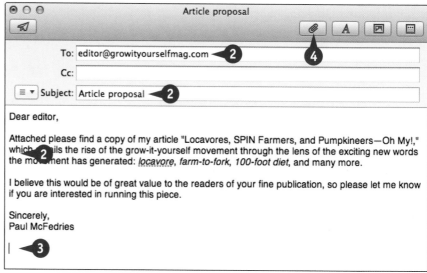

A message window appears.

2 Fill in the recipients, subject, and message text as described in the previous section.

3 Press Return two or three times to move the cursor a few lines below your message.

4 Click **Attach** (📎).

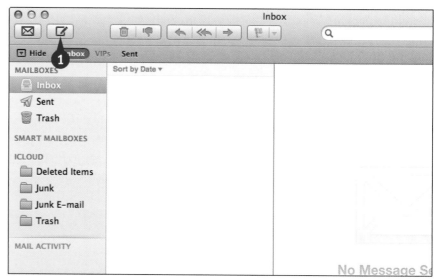

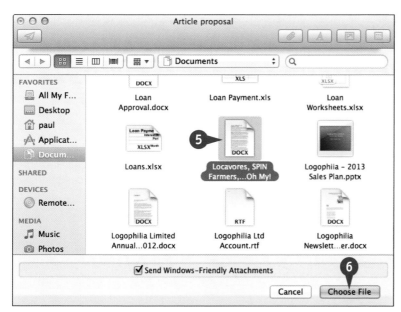

A file selection dialog appears.

5 Click the file you want to attach.

6 Click **Choose File**.

A Mail attaches the file to the message.

Note: *Another way to attach a file to a message is to click and drag the file from Finder and drop it inside the message.*

7 Repeat Steps **4** to **6** to attach additional files to the message.

8 Click **Send** (📨).

Mail sends your message.

Is there a limit to the number of files I can attach to a message?
The number of files you can attach to the message has no practical limit. However, you should be careful with the total *size* of the files you send to someone. If either of you have a slow Internet connection, then sending or receiving the message can take an extremely long time. Also, many ISPs place a limit on the size of a message's attachments, which is usually between 2MB and 5MB. In general, use e-mail to send only a few small files at a time.

Add a Signature

In an e-mail message, a *signature* is a small amount of text that appears at the bottom of the message. Instead of typing this information manually in each message, you can save the signature in your Mail preferences. When you compose a new e-mail message, reply to an existing message, or forward a message, you can click a button to have Mail add the signature to your outgoing message.

Signatures usually contain personal contact information, such as your phone numbers, business address, and e-mail and website addresses.

Add a Signature

Create a Signature

1 Click **Mail**.

2 Click **Preferences**.

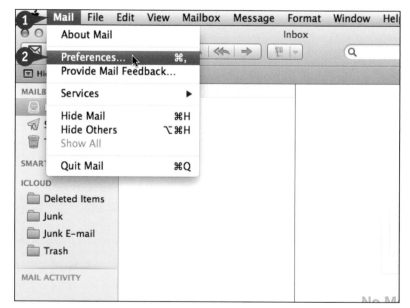

The Mail preferences appear.

3 Click **Signatures**.

4 Click the account for which you want to use the signature.

5 Click **Create a signature** (⊞).

Mail adds a new signature.

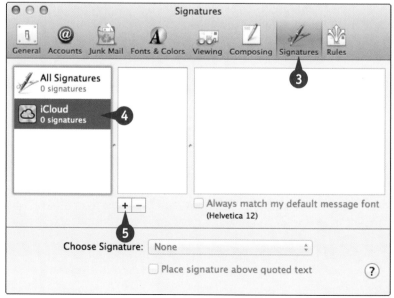

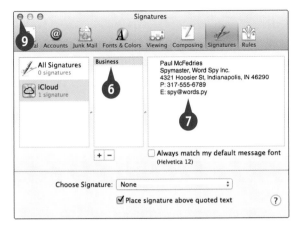

6 Type a name for the signature.

7 Type the signature text.

8 Repeat Steps **4** to **7** to add other signatures, if required.

Note: *You can add as many signatures as you want. For example, you may want to have one signature for business use and another for personal use.*

9 Click 🔘.

Insert the Signature

1 Click **New Message** (🖉) to start a new message.

Note: *To start a new message, see the section "Send an E-mail Message."*

2 In the message text area, move the insertion point to the location where you want the signature to appear.

3 Click the **Signature** ⬚ and then click the signature you want to insert.

A The signature appears in the message.

---

simplify it

When I have multiple signatures, how can I choose which of them Mail adds automatically?

1 Follow Steps **1** to **4** to display the signature preferences and choose an account.

2 Click ⬚ and then click the signature you want to insert automatically into each message.

A If you prefer to add a signature manually, click **None** instead of a signature.

3 Click 🔘.

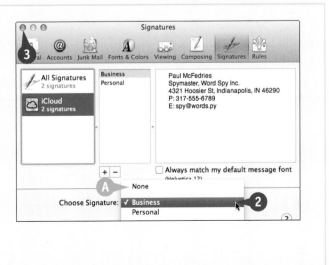

Receive and Read E-mail Messages

When another person sends you an e-mail message, that message ends up in your e-mail account's mailbox on the incoming mail server maintained by your ISP or e-mail provider. However, that company does not automatically pass along that message to you. Instead, you must use Mail to connect to your mailbox on the incoming mail server and then retrieve any messages waiting for you. By default, Mail automatically checks for new messages every 5 minutes while you are online, but you can also check for new messages at any time.

Receive and Read E-mail Messages

Receive E-mail Messages

1 Click **Get Mail** (✉).

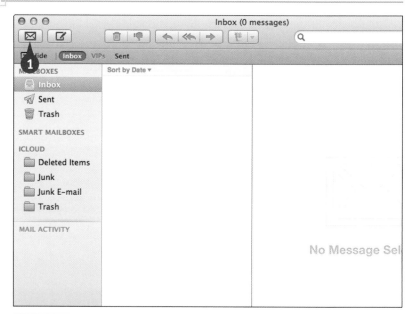

A The Mail Activity area lets you know if you have any incoming messages.

B If you have new messages, they appear in your Inbox folder with a blue dot in this column.

C The 🖼 icon in the Dock shows the number of unread messages in the Inbox folder.

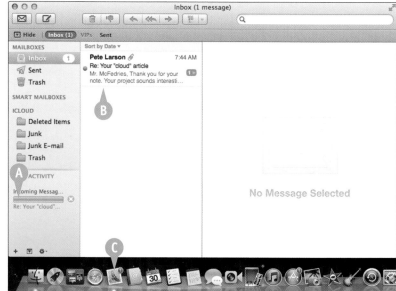

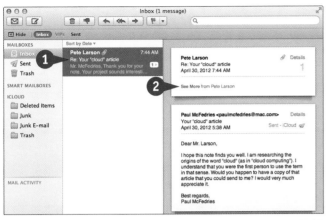

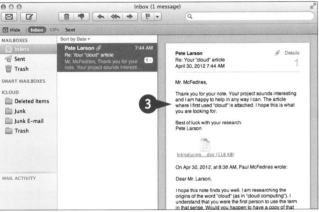

Read a Message

1 Click the message.

2 If you do not see the full message, click **See more**.

3 Read the message text in the preview pane.

Note: *If you want to open the message in its own window, double-click the message.*

Can I change how often Mail automatically checks for messages?
Yes, by following these steps:

1 Click **Mail**.

2 Click **Preferences**.

The Mail preferences appear.

3 Click the **General** tab.

4 In the Check for new messages pop-up menu, click ⊟ and then click the time interval that you want Mail to use when checking for new messages automatically.

Ⓐ If you do not want Mail to check for messages automatically, click **Manually** instead.

5 Click ⊙.

Reply to a Message

When a message you receive requires some kind of response — whether it is answering a question, supplying information, or providing comments — you can reply to that message. Most replies go only to the person who sent the original message. However, it is also possible to send the reply to all the people who were included in the original message's To and Cc lines. Mail includes the text of the original message in the reply, but you should edit the original message text to include only enough of the original message to put your reply into context.

Reply to a Message

1. Click the message to which you want to reply.

2. Click the reply type you want to use.

   Click **Reply** (⬑) to respond only to the person who sent the message.

   Click **Reply All** (⬱) to respond to all the addresses in the message's From, To, and Cc lines.

   A message window appears.

Ⓐ Mail automatically inserts the recipient addresses.

Ⓑ Mail also inserts the subject line, preceded by Re:.

Ⓒ Mail includes the original message text at the bottom of the reply.

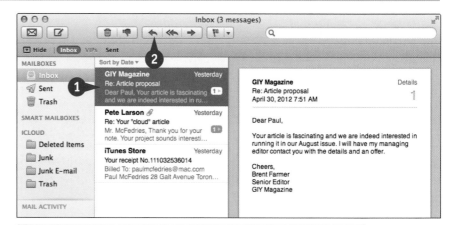

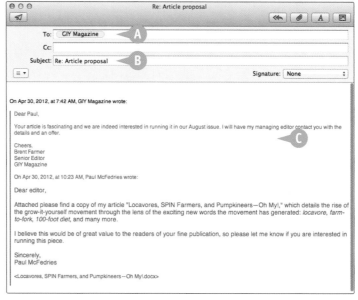

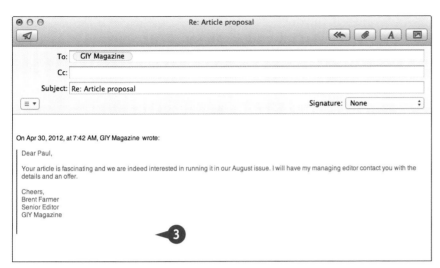

❸ Edit the original message to include only the text that is relevant to your reply.

❹ Click the area above the original message text and type your reply.

❺ Click **Send** (📨).

Mail sends your reply.

Note: *Mail stores a copy of your reply in the Sent folder.*

I received a message inadvertently. Is there a way that I can pass it along to the correct recipient?
Yes. Click the message that you received inadvertently, click **Message**, and then click **Redirect** (or press Shift + ⌘ + E). Type the recipient's address and then click **Send**. Replies to this message will be sent to the original sender, not to you.

How much of the original message should I include in my reply?
If the original message is fairly short, you usually do not need to edit the text. However, if the original message is long, and your response deals only with part of that message, you will save the recipient time and confusion by deleting everything except the relevant portion of the text.

Forward a Message

If a message has information relevant to or that concerns another person, you can forward a copy of the message to that person. You can also include your own comments in the forward.

In the body of the forward, Mail includes the original message's addresses, date, and subject line. Below this information Mail also includes the text of the original message. In most cases you will leave the entire message intact so your recipient can see it. However, if only part of the message is relevant to the recipient, you should edit the original message accordingly.

Forward a Message

1 Click the message that you want to forward.

2 Click **Forward** (➡).

Note: *You can also press* Shift + ⌘ + F .

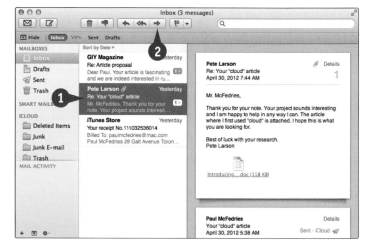

A message window appears.

A Mail inserts the subject line, preceded by Fwd:.

B The original message's addressees (To and From), date, subject, and text are included at the top of the forward.

3 Type the e-mail address of the person to whom you are forwarding the message.

4 To send a copy of the forward to another person, type that person's e-mail address in the Cc line.

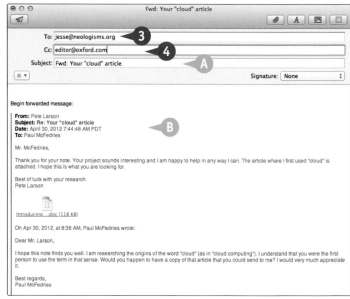

5 Edit the original message to include only the text that is relevant to your forward.

6 Click the area above the original message text and type your comments.

7 Click **Send** (📮).

Mail sends your forward.

Note: *Mail stores a copy of your forward in the Sent folder.*

Note: *You can forward someone a copy of the actual message instead of just a copy of the message text. Click the message, click **Message**, and then click **Forward As Attachment**. Mail creates a new message and includes the original message as an attachment.*

Mail always formats my replies as rich text, even when the original message is plain text. How can I fix this problem?

You can configure Mail to always reply using the same format as the original message. Follow these steps:

1 Click **Mail**.

2 Click **Preferences**.

The Mail preferences appear.

3 Click the **Composing** tab.

4 Click the **Use the same message format as the original message** check box (☐ changes to ☑).

5 Click 🔘.

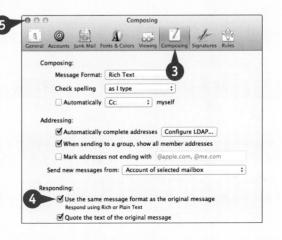

Open and Save
an Attachment

If you receive a message that has a file attached, you can open the attachment to view the contents of the file. You can also save the attachment as a file on your Mac.

Some files that you receive as e-mail attachments only require a quick viewing, so you can open these files and then close them when you are done. Other attachments may contain information that you want to keep, so you should save these files to your Mac's hard disk. Be careful when dealing with attached files. Computer viruses are often transmitted by e-mail attachments.

Open and Save an Attachment

Open An Attachment

1 Click the message that has the attachment, as indicated by the **Attachment** symbol (🖉).

A An icon appears for each message attachment.

2 Double-click the attachment you want to open.

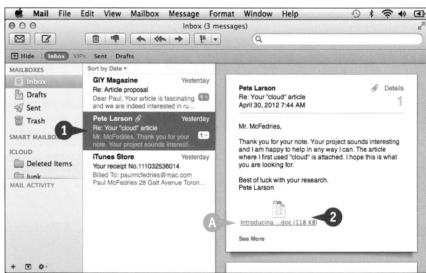

The file opens in the associated application.

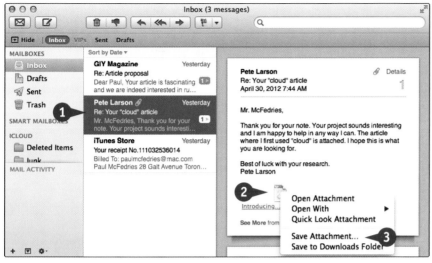

Save An Attachment

1 Click the message that has the attachment, as indicated by the Attachment symbol (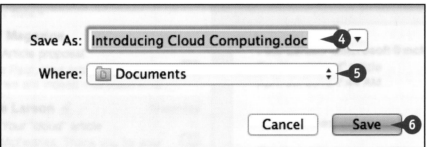).

2 Right-click the attachment you want to save.

3 Click **Save Attachment**.

Mail prompts you to save the file.

4 Click in the **Save As** text box and edit the filename, if desired.

5 Click the arrows (⊟) and select the folder into which you want the file saved.

6 Click **Save**.

Can I open an attachment using a different application?
In most cases, yes. OS X usually has a default application that it uses when you double-click a file attachment. However, it also usually defines one or more other applications that are capable of opening the file. To check this out, right-click the icon of the attachment you want to open and then click **Open With**. In the menu that appears, click the application that you prefer to use to open the file.

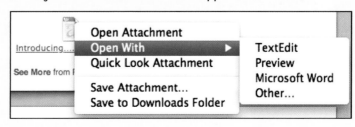

Create a Mailbox for Saving Messages

After you have used Mail for a while, you may find that you have many messages in your Inbox. To keep the Inbox uncluttered, you can create new mailboxes and then move messages from the Inbox to the new mailboxes.

You should use each mailbox you create to save related messages. For example, you could create separate mailboxes for people you correspond with regularly, projects you are working on, different work departments, and so on.

Create a Mailbox for Saving Messages

Create a Mailbox

① Click **Mailbox**.

② Click **New Mailbox**.

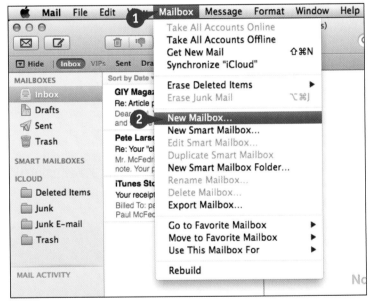

The New Mailbox dialog appears.

③ Click the **Location** ⊟ and then click where you want the mailbox located.

④ Type the name of the new mailbox.

⑤ Click **OK**.

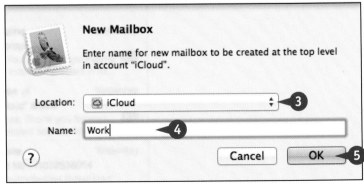

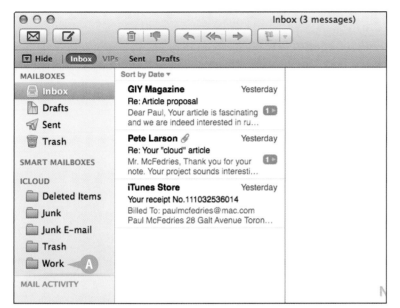

A The new mailbox appears in the Mailbox list.

Move a Message to Another Mailbox

1 Position the mouse ▸ over the message you want to move.

2 Click and drag the message and drop it on the mailbox to which you want to move it.

Mail moves the message.

How do I rename a mailbox?
Right-click the mailbox and then click **Rename Mailbox**. Type the new name and then press `Return`. Note that Mail does not allow you to rename any of the built-in mailboxes, including Inbox, Drafts, and Trash.

How do I delete a mailbox?
Right-click the mailbox and then click **Delete**. When Mail asks you to confirm the deletion, click **Delete**. Note that Mail does not allow you to delete any of the built-in mailboxes, including Inbox, Drafts, and Trash. Remember, too, that when you delete a mailbox, you also delete any messages stored in that mailbox.

CHAPTER 6

Talking via Messages and FaceTime

OS X Mountain Lion comes with the Messages application, which you use to exchange instant messages with other users of OS X Mountain Lion, as well as anyone with an iPhone, iPad, or iPod touch. You can also use the FaceTime application if you want to make video calls to other people. This chapter shows you how to perform these communications tasks.

Configure Messages

OS X Mountain Lion includes the Messages application to enable you to exchange instant messages with other people who are online. The first time you open Messages, you must run through a short configuration process to set up your account.

This process involves signing in with your Apple ID and deciding whether you want Messages to send out notifications that tell people when you have read the messages they send to you.

Configure Messages

1 Click **Messages** (🗨).

The Welcome to Messages dialog appears.

2 Click **Continue**.

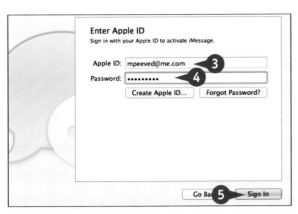

The iMessage Setup dialog appears.

③ Type your Apple ID.

④ Type your Apple ID password.

⑤ Click **Sign In**.

⑥ If you want other people to know when you have read their message, click **Send read receipts** (☐ changes to ☑).

⑦ Click **Continue**.

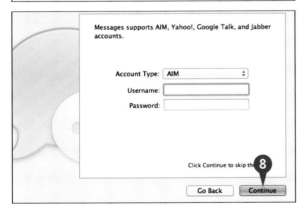

The Account Setup dialog appears.

⑧ Click **Continue**.

⑨ Click **Done**.

Messages is now ready to use.

simplify it

What if I do not have an Apple ID?
You can create a new Apple ID during the configuration process. Follow Steps 1 and 2 to open the iMessage Setup dialog, and then click **Create Apple ID**. In the dialog that appears, type your name, the e-mail address you want to use as your Apple ID, and the password you want to use. You must also choose a secret question and specify your birthday. Click **Create Apple ID** to complete the operation.

Send a Message

In the Messages application, an instant messaging conversation is most often the exchange of text messages between two or more people who are online and available to chat.

An instant messaging conversation begins by one person inviting another person to exchange messages. In Messages, this means sending an initial instant message, and the recipient either accepts or rejects the invitation.

Send a Message

1 Click **Compose new message** (☑).

Note: *You can also click* ***File*** *and then click* ***New Message***, *or press* ⌘+Ⓝ.

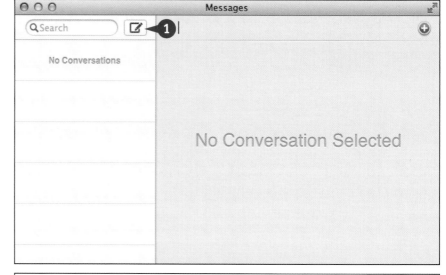

Messages begins a new conversation.

2 In the To field, type the message recipient using one of the following:

The person's e-mail address.

The person's mobile phone number.

The person's name, if that person is in your Contacts list.

Ⓐ You can also click **Add Contact** (◎) to select a name from your Contacts list.

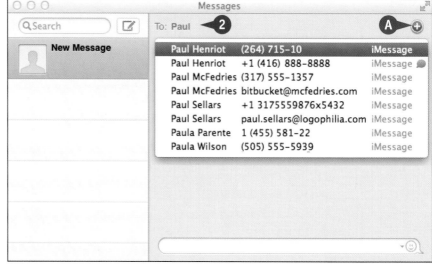

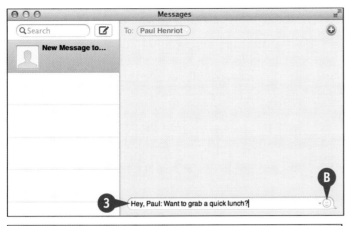

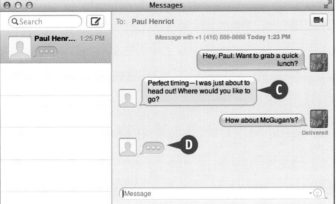

3 Type your message.

B You can also click here if you want to insert a smiley symbol into your message.

4 Press Return.

Messages sends the text to the recipient.

C The recipient's response appears in the transcript window.

D You see the ellipsis symbol (⬚) when the other person is typing.

5 Repeat Steps 3 and 4 to continue the conversation.

simplify it

Can I change my picture?
Yes. Click **Messages** and then click **Change My Picture**. In the Edit Picture dialog that appears, select a category (such as Defaults for the OS X default account images, or Other to choose one of your own images), select the picture, and then click **Done**.

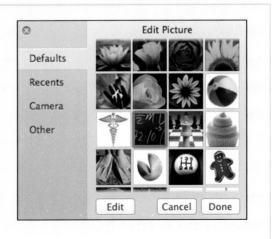

Send a File
in a Message

If during an instant messaging conversation you realize you need to send someone a file, you can save time by sending the file directly from the Messages application.

When you need to send a file to another person, your first thought might be to attach that file to an

e-mail message, as described in Chapter 5. However, if you happen to be in the middle of an instant messaging conversation with that person, it is easier and faster to use Messages to send the file.

Send a File in a Message

① Start the conversation with the person to whom you want to send the file.

② Click **Buddies**.

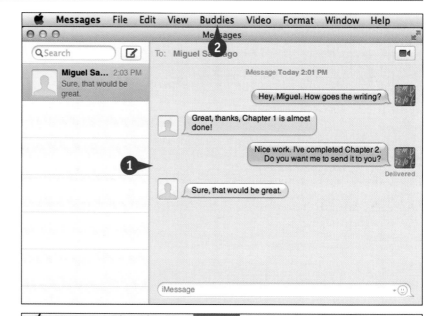

③ Click **Send File**.

Note: *You can also press* Option + ⌘ + F.

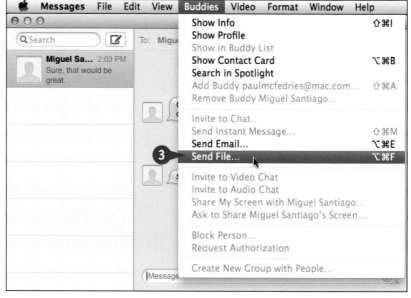

Messages displays a file selection dialog.

④ Click the file you want to send.

⑤ Click **Send**.

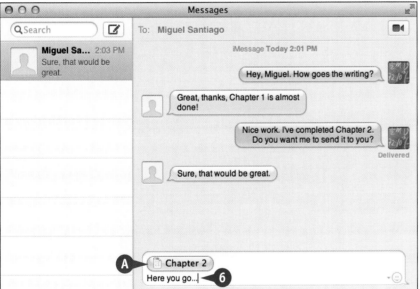

Ⓐ Messages adds an icon for the file to the message box.

⑥ Type your message.

⑦ Press Return.

Messages sends the message and adds the file as an attachment.

How do I save a file that I receive during a conversation?

When you receive a message that has a file attachment, the message shows the name of the file, with the file's type icon to the left and a downward-pointing arrow (⊙) to the right.

Click ⊙ to save the file to your Downloads folder.

Messages saves the file and then displays the Downloads folder.

iMessage Today 3:13 PM

🖼 Urban Garden Design ⊙
Thought you might like this...

Open and Close FaceTime

OS X Mountain Lion comes with a video chat feature called FaceTime that enables you to see and speak to another person over the Internet. To use FaceTime, you and your friend must have the right type of equipment. If either or both of you are using a Mac, you must have a web camera attached to the computer, such as the iSight or FaceTime HD camera that comes with many Macs, and you must have a microphone attached to the computer. After you have all the necessary equipment, you must first learn how to open and close FaceTime.

Open and Close FaceTime

Open FaceTime

1 In the Dock, click **FaceTime** (☉).

The FaceTime window appears.

Close FaceTime

1 Click **FaceTime**.

2 Click **Quit FaceTime**.

OS X shuts down the FaceTime application.

simplify it

Are there other methods I can use to open FaceTime?
Yes. If you do not have 🔲 in the Dock, there are a couple of methods you can use to open FaceTime. If you have used FaceTime recently, a reasonably fast method is to click 🍎, click **Recent Items**, and then click **FaceTime**. Alternatively, click **Spotlight** (🔍), type **facetime**, and then click **FaceTime** in the search results. If you want to switch an instant messaging conversation to a FaceTime conversation, click the **FaceTime** icon (🎦) in the Messages window.

Sign In to FaceTime

To use FaceTime to conduct video chats with your friends, you must each first sign in using your Apple ID. This could be an iCloud account that uses the Apple me.com address, or it could be your existing e-mail address.

After you have created your Apple ID, you can use it to sign in to FaceTime. Note that you only have to do this once. In subsequent sessions, FaceTime automatically signs you in.

Sign In to FaceTime

1 In the Dock, click **FaceTime** (📷).

2 Type your Apple ID e-mail address.

3 Type your Apple ID password.

4 Click **Sign In**.

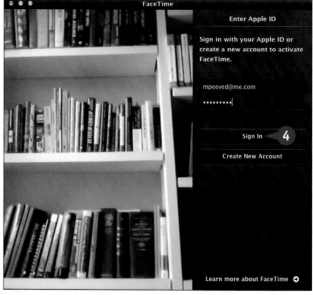

FaceTime prompts you to specify an e-mail address that people can use to contact you via FaceTime.

⑤ If the address you prefer to use is different from your Apple ID, type the address you want to use.

⑥ Click **Next**.

FaceTime verifies your Apple ID and then displays a list of contacts.

Which devices support FaceTime?

You can use the FaceTime application on any Mac that is running OS X 10.6.6 or later. For OS X Snow Leopard (10.6.6), FaceTime is available through the App Store for 99 cents. For OS X Mountain Lion (10.8) and OS X Lion (10.7), FaceTime is installed by default. The FaceTime software is also available as an app that runs on the iPhone 4 and later, the iPad 2 and later, and the iPod touch fourth generation and later.

Connect Through FaceTime

After you have signed in with your Apple ID, you can use the FaceTime application to connect with another person and conduct a video chat. How you connect with the other person depends on what device he or she is using for FaceTime. If the person is using a Mac, an iPad, or an iPod touch, you can use whatever e-mail address the person has designated as his or her FaceTime contact address. If the person is using an iPhone 4 or later, you can use that person's mobile number to make the connection.

Connect Through FaceTime

1 Click **Contacts**.

2 Click the contact you want to call.

FaceTime displays the contact's data.

3 Click the phone number (for an iPhone) or e-mail address (for a Mac, iPad, or iPod touch) that you want to use to connect to the contact.

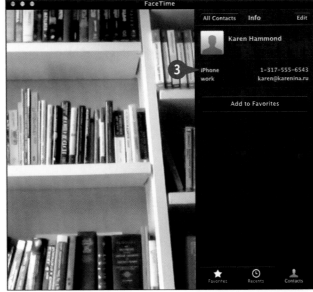

FaceTime sends a message to the contact asking if he or she would like a FaceTime connection.

④ The other person must click or tap **Accept** to complete the connection.

FaceTime connects with the other person.

Ⓐ The other person's video takes up the bulk of the FaceTime screen.

Ⓑ Your video appears in the picture-in-picture (PiP) window.

Note: *You can click and drag the PiP to a different location within the FaceTime window.*

⑤ When you have finished your FaceTime call, click **End**.

Are there easier ways to connect to someone through FaceTime?
Yes, FaceTime offers a couple of methods that you might find faster. If you have connected with a person through FaceTime recently, that person may appear in the FaceTime Recents list. In the FaceTime window, click **Recents** and then click the person you want to contact.

Alternatively, if you connect with someone frequently, you can add that person to the FaceTime Favorites list. Use the Contacts list to click the person, and then click **Add to Favorites**. To connect with a favorite, click **Favorites** and then click the person.

CHAPTER 7

Tracking Your Contacts and Events

You may find that your life is busier than ever, and the number of people you need to stay in touch with, events you have to keep track of, and tasks you have to perform seem to increase daily. Fortunately, OS X comes with two applications that can help you manage your busy life. You use the Contacts application to manage your contacts by storing information such as phone numbers, e-mail addresses, street addresses, and much more. You use the Calendar application to enter and track events and to-do items.

Open and Close Contacts

OS X includes the Contacts application to enable you to manage information about the people you know, whether they are colleagues, friends, or family members. The Contacts app refers to these people as *contacts*, and you store each person's data in an object called a *card*.

Before you can add or work with your contacts, you must know how to start the Contacts application. When you are finished with Contacts, you should close it to reduce desktop clutter and save system resources.

Open and Close Contacts

Open Contacts

1 In the Dock, click **Contacts** (📖).

The Contacts window appears.

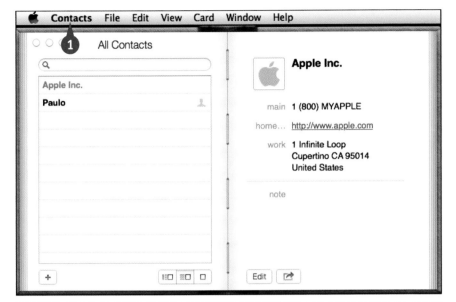

Close Contacts

1 Click **Contacts**.

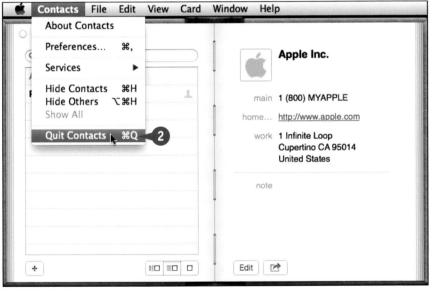

2 Click **Quit Contacts**.

Are there other methods I can use to open Contacts?
Yes. If you have removed the  icon from the Dock, there are a couple of other quick methods you can use to start Contacts. If you have used Contacts recently, click the **Apple** icon (),
click **Recent Items**, and
then click **Contacts**. You can
also click **Spotlight** (), type
contacts, and then click
Contacts in the search results.

Add a New Contact

To store contact information for a particular person, you first need to create a new contact within Contacts. You do that by creating a new card, which is a Contacts item that stores data about a person or company.

Each card can store a wide variety of information. For example, you can store a person's name, company name, phone numbers, e-mail address, instant messaging data, street address, notes, and much more. Although you will mostly use Contacts cards to store data about people, you can also use a card to keep information about companies.

Add a New Contact

1. Click **File**.

2. Click **New Card**.

Ⓐ You can also begin a new contact by clicking ⊞.

Note: *You can also invoke the New Card command by pressing* ⌘+N.

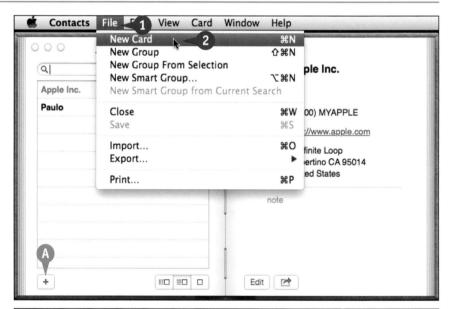

Ⓑ Contacts adds a new card.

3. In the First field, type the contact's first name.

4. In the Last field, type the contact's last name.

5. In the Company field, type the contact's company name.

6. If the contact is a company, click **Company** (☐ changes to ☑).

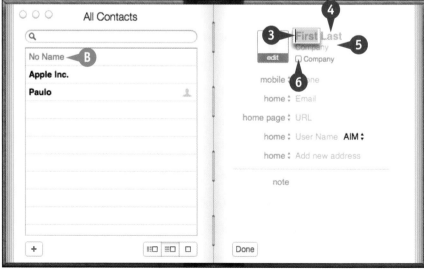

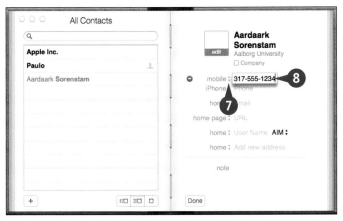

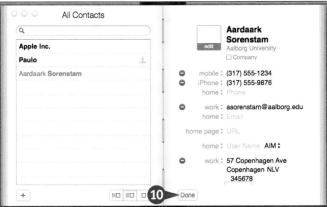

7 In the first Phone field, click ⊡ and then click the category you want to use.

8 Type the phone number.

9 Repeat Steps **7** and **8** to enter data in some or all of the other fields.

Note: *To learn how to add more fields to the card, see the "Edit a Contact" section.*

10 Click **Done**.

Contacts saves the new card.

If I include a contact's e-mail address, is there a way to send that person a message without having to type the address?
Yes. You can follow these steps:

1 Click the contact's card.

2 Click the e-mail address category.

3 Click **Send Email**.

Apple Mail displays a new e-mail message with the contact already added in the To line.

4 Fill in the rest of the message as required.

5 Click **Send**.

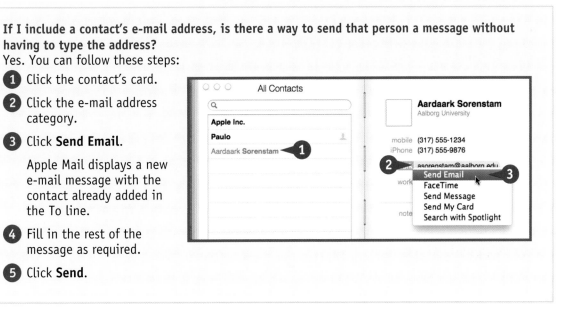

Edit a Contact

If you need to make changes to the information already in a contact's card, or if you need to add new information to a card, you can edit the card from within Contacts. The default fields you see in a card are not the only types of data you can store for a contact. Contacts offers a large number of extra fields. These include useful fields such as Middle Name, Nickname, Job Title, Department, URL (web address), and Birthday. You can also add extra fields for common data items such as phone numbers, e-mail addresses, and dates.

Edit a Contact

① Click the card you want to edit.

② Click **Edit**.

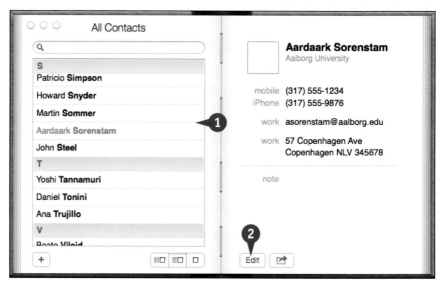

Ⓐ Contacts makes the card's fields available for editing.

③ Edit the existing fields as required.

④ To add a field, click an empty placeholder and then type the field data.

⑤ To remove a field, click ⊖.

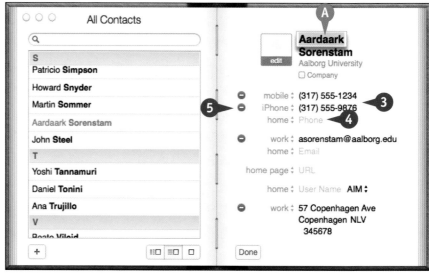

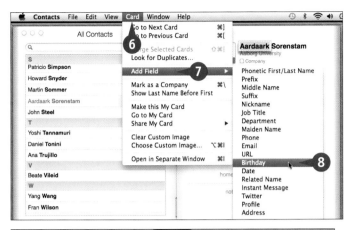

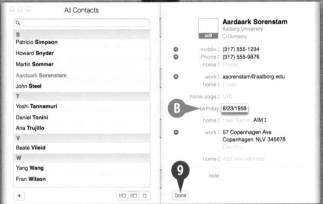

⑥ To add a new field type, click **Card**.

⑦ Click **Add Field**.

⑧ Click the type of field you want.

Ⓑ Contacts adds the field to the card.

⑨ When you have completed your edits, click **Done**.

Contacts saves the edited card.

How do I add a picture for the new contact?
Follow these steps:

① Click the contact's card.

② Click **Edit**.

③ Double-click the picture box.

④ Click the type of picture you want to add.

⑤ Click the picture.

⑥ Click **Done**.

⑦ Click **Done**.

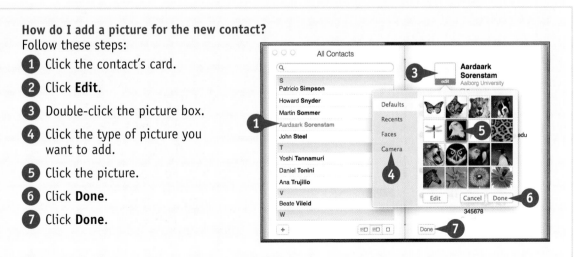

Create a Contact Group

You can organize your contacts into one or more groups, which is useful if you want to view just a subset of your contacts. For example, you could create separate groups for friends, family members, work colleagues, or business clients.

Groups are particularly handy if you have a large number of contacts in your address book. By creating

and maintaining groups, you can navigate your contacts more easily. You can also perform groupwide tasks, such as sending a single e-mail message to everyone in the group. You can create a group first and then add members, or you can select members in advance and then create the group.

Create a Contact Group

Create a Contact Group

1 Click **File**.

2 Click **New Group**.

Note: *You can also run the New Group command by pressing* Shift+⌘+N.

A Contacts adds a new group.

3 Type a name for the group.

4 Press Return.

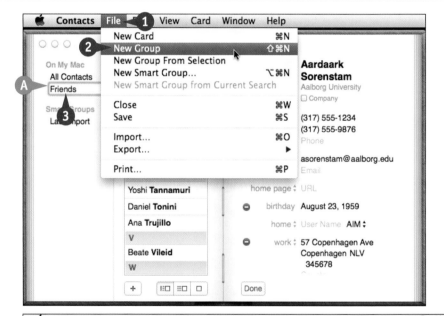

5 Click and drag a contact to the group.

Contacts adds the contact to the group.

6 Repeat Step 5 for the other contacts you want to add to the group.

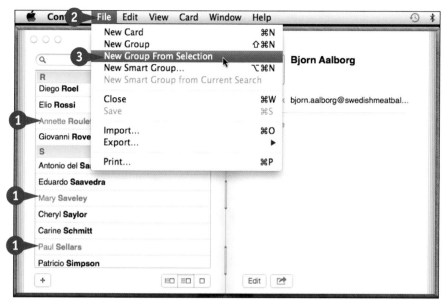

Create a Group of Selected Contacts

1 Select the contacts you want to include in the new group.

Note: *To select multiple contacts, press and hold* ⌘ *and click each card.*

2 Click **File**.

3 Click **New Group From Selection**.

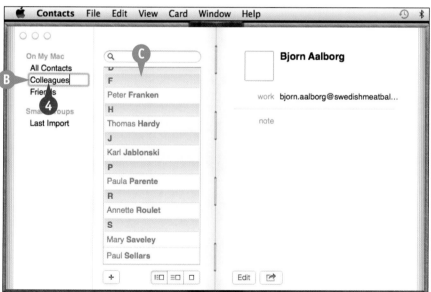

B Contacts adds a new group.

C Contacts adds the selected contacts as group members.

4 Type a name for the group.

5 Press Return.

Can I send an e-mail message to the group?
Yes. Normally, sending an e-mail message to multiple contacts involves typing or selecting multiple addresses. With a group, you send a single message to the group, and Mail automatically sends a copy to each member. Right-click the group and then click **Send Email to "*Group*"** where *Group* is the name of the group.

What is a smart group?
A *smart group* is a special group where each member has one or more fields in common, such as the company name, department name, city, or state. When you create the smart group, you specify one or more criteria, and then Contacts automatically adds members to the group if they meet those criteria. To create a smart group, click **File**, click **New Smart Group**, and then enter your group criteria.

Open and Close Calendar

Your Mac comes with the Calendar application to enable you to manage your schedule. Calendar enables you to create and work with events, which are either scheduled appointments such as meetings, lunches, and visits to the dentist, or all-day activities, such as birthdays, anniversaries, or vacations. You can also use Calendar to send event

invitations and to accept or decline any event invitations that you receive.

Before you can add or work with events (appointments, meetings, all-day activities, and so on), and before you can send or accept event invitations, you must know how to start the Calendar application.

Open and Close Calendar

Open Calendar

1 In the Dock, click **Calendar** (📅).

The Calendar window appears.

Close Calendar

1 Click **Calendar**.

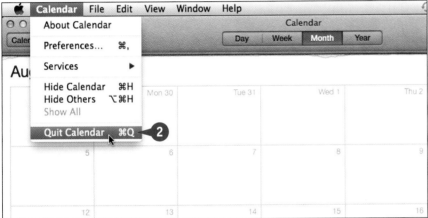

2 Click **Quit Calendar**.

Are there other methods I can use to open Calendar?
Yes. If you have removed the 📅 icon from the Dock, there are a couple of other quick methods you can use to start Calendar. If you have used Calendar recently, a reasonably fast method is to click 🍎, click **Recent Items**, and then click **Calendar**. You can also click **Spotlight** (🔍), type **cal**, and then click **Calendar** in the search results.

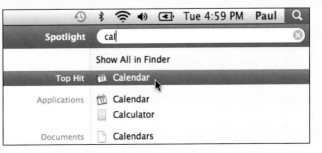

Navigate the Calendar

Before you create an event such as a meeting, or an all-day event such as a conference, you must first select the date when the event occurs. You can do this in Calendar by navigating the built-in calendar or by specifying the date.

Calendar also lets you change the calendar view to suit your needs. For example, you can show just a single day's worth of events if you want to concentrate on that day's activities. Similarly, you can view a week's worth of events if you want to get a larger sense of what your overall schedule looks like.

Navigate the Calendar

Use the Calendar

1 Click **Month**.

2 Click the **Next Month** button (▶) until the month of your event appears.

A If you go too far, click the **Previous Month** button (◀) to move back to the month you want.

B To see a specific date, click the day and then click **Day** (or press ⌘+①).

C To see a specific week, click any day within the week and then click **Week** (or press ⌘+②).

D To return to viewing the entire month, click **Month** (or press ⌘+③).

E If you want to return to today's date, click **Today** (or press ⌘+T).

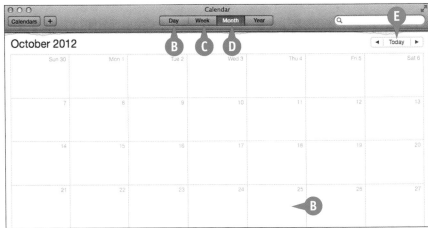

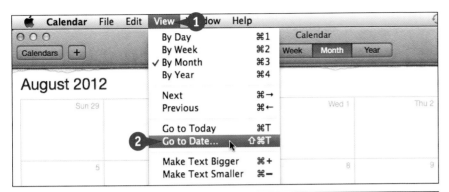

Go to a Specific Date

1 Click **View**.

2 Click **Go to Date**.

Note: *You can also select the Go to Date command by pressing* Shift+⌘+T.

The Go to date dialog appears.

3 In the Date text box, type the date you want using the format mm/dd/yyyy.

F You can also click the month, day, or year and then click ⊟ to increase or decrease the value.

4 Click **Show**.

5 Click **Day**.

G Calendar displays the date.

In the Week view, the week begins on Sunday. How can I change this to Monday?
Calendar's default Week view has Sunday on the left and Saturday on the right. To display the

weekend days together with Monday on the left signaling the start of the week, follow these steps:

1 Click **Calendar** in the menu bar.

2 Click **Preferences**.

3 Click the **General** tab.

4 Click the **Start week on** ⊟ and select **Monday** from the pop-up menu.

5 Click ⊙.

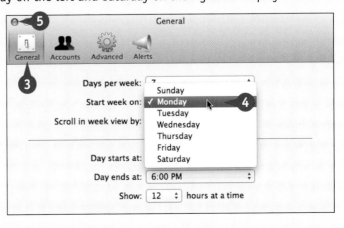

Create
an Event

You can help organize your life by using Calendar to record your events — such as appointments, meetings, phone calls, and dates — on the date and time they occur.

If the event has a set time and duration — for example, a meeting or a lunch date — you add

the event directly to the calendar as a regular appointment. If the event has no set time — for example, a birthday, anniversary, or multiple-day event such as a convention or vacation — you can create an all-day event.

Create an Event

Create a Regular Event

① Navigate to the date when the event occurs.

② Click **Calendars**.

③ Click the calendar you want to use.

④ Double-click the time when the event starts.

Ⓐ Calendar adds a one-hour event.

Note: *If the event is less than or more than an hour, you can also click and drag the mouse ► over the full event period.*

⑤ Type the name of the event.

⑥ Press Return.

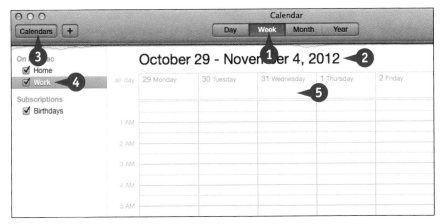

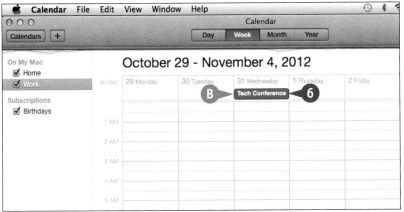

Create an All-Day Event

① Click **Week**.

② Navigate to the week that includes the date when the event occurs.

③ Click **Calendars**.

④ Click the calendar you want to use.

⑤ Double-click anywhere inside the event date's all-day section.

Ⓑ Calendar adds a new all-day event.

⑥ Type the name of the event.

⑦ Press Return.

How can I specify event details such as the location and a reminder message?

① Follow the steps in this section to create an event.

② Double-click the event.

③ Click **Edit** (☐ changes to ☑).

④ Type the location of the event in the location text box.

⑤ Click the **Alert** ☐ and select **Message** from the pop-up menu.

⑥ Click the **Alert** ☐ and select the amount of time before the event that you want to receive the reminder.

⑦ Click **Done**.

Calendar saves the new event configuration.

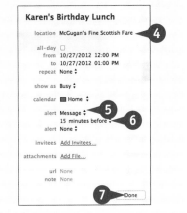

Create a Repeating Event

If you have an activity or event that recurs at a regular interval, you can create an event and configure it to repeat in Calendar automatically. This saves you from having to add the future events repeatedly yourself because Calendar adds them for you automatically.

You can repeat an event daily, weekly, monthly, or yearly. For even greater flexibility, you can set up a custom interval. For example, you could have an event repeat every five days, every second Friday, on the first Monday of every month, and so on.

Create a Repeating Event

1 Follow the steps in the previous section to create an event.

2 Double-click the event.

Calendar displays information for the event.

3 Click **Edit**.

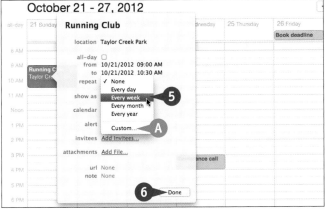

Calendar opens the event for editing.

④ Beside the repeat label, click **None** ⬍.

⑤ Click the interval you want to use.

Ⓐ If you want to specify a custom interval such as every two weeks or the first Monday of every month, click **Custom** and configure your interval in the dialog that appears.

⑥ Click **Done**.

Calendar adds the repeating events to the calendar.

---

simplify it

How do I configure an event to stop after a certain number of occurrences?

① Follow Steps **1** to **5** to select a recurrence interval.

② Beside the end label, click **None** ⬍ and then click **After** from the pop-up menu.

③ Type the number of occurrences you want.

④ Click **Done**.

Can I delete a single occurrence from a recurring series of events?
Yes, you can delete one occurrence from the calendar without affecting the rest of the series. Click the occurrence you want to delete, and then press Del. Calendar asks whether you want to delete all the occurrences or just the selected occurrence. Click **Delete Only This Event**.

CHAPTER 8

Playing and Organizing Music

Using iTunes, you can create a library of music and use that library to play songs, albums, and collections of songs called playlists. You can also use iTunes to listen to music CDs, import tracks from music CDs, create your own CDs, and more. You can also purchase music from the online iTunes Store, tune in to an Internet radio station, and subscribe to podcasts.

Open and Close iTunes

Your Mac includes iTunes to enable you to play back and manage various types of audio files. iTunes also includes features for organizing and playing videos, watching movies and TV shows, and organizing e-books, but this chapter focuses on the audio features in iTunes.

To begin using the program, you must first learn how to find and open the iTunes window. When you finish using the program, you can close the iTunes window to free up computer processing power.

Open and Close iTunes

Open iTunes

1 In the Dock, click **iTunes** (◉).

The iTunes window appears.

Close iTunes

① Click **iTunes**.

② Click **Quit iTunes**.

Are there other methods I can use to open iTunes?

Yes. If you have removed the 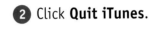 icon from the Dock, there are a couple of other quick methods you can use to start iTunes. If you have used iTunes recently, a reasonably fast method is to click the Apple icon (), click **Recent Items**, and then click **iTunes**. You can also click **Spotlight** (), type **itunes**, and then click **iTunes** in the search results.

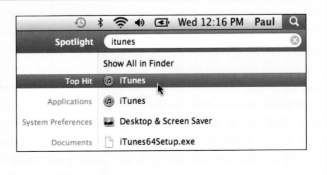

Understanding the iTunes Library

Most of your iTunes time will be spent in the Library, so you need to understand what the Library is and how you work with it. In particular, you need to understand the various categories — such as music and audiobooks — that iTunes uses to organize the Library's audio content. In addition, to make it easier to navigate the Library, you need to know how to configure the Library to show only the categories with which you will be working.

The iTunes Library

The iTunes Library is where your Mac stores the files that you can play and work with in the iTunes application. Although iTunes has some video components, its focus is on audio features, so most of the Library sections are audio-related. These sections enable you to work with music, podcasts, audiobooks, ringtones, and Internet radio.

Understanding Library Categories

The left side of the iTunes window is called the Source List. It displays the various categories that are available in the iTunes Library. In the Library list, the audio-related categories include Music, Podcasts, Books (for audiobooks), Ringtones, and Radio. The Store list includes items you have purchased from the iTunes Store.

Each category shows you the contents of that category and the details for each item. For example, in the Music category, you can see details such as the name of each album and the artist who recorded it.

Configuring the Library

You can configure which categories of the iTunes Library appear in the Library list on the left side of the iTunes window. Click **iTunes** and then click **Preferences** to open the iTunes preferences; then click the **General** tab. In the Show section, click the check box for each type of content you want to work with (☐ changes to ☑), and then click **OK**.

Navigate the iTunes Window

Familiarizing yourself with the various elements of the iTunes window is a good idea so that you can easily navigate and activate elements when you are ready to play audio files, music CDs, or podcasts; import and burn audio CDs; create your own playlists; or listen to Internet radio.

In particular, you need to learn the iTunes playback controls, because you will use them to control the playback of almost all music you work with in iTunes. It is also worthwhile to learn the different View options, because these often come in handy when navigating the iTunes Library.

Ⓐ Playback Controls

These buttons control media playback and enable you to adjust the volume.

Ⓑ Sort Buttons

These buttons sort the contents of the current iTunes category.

Ⓒ Status Area

This area displays information about the item that is currently playing or the action that iTunes is currently performing.

Ⓓ View Options

These buttons control how the contents of the current category appear. Click **List** (▤) to view the contents as a list by song; click **Album List** (▦) to view the contents as a list by album; click **Grid** (▦) to view the contents as thumbnails; click **Cover Flow** (▦) to view the contents as scrolling thumbnails.

Ⓔ Genius Sidebar

This area displays a list of songs, albums, or other iTunes Store content similar to the current item in the Library. Click **Store** and then click **Turn On Genius** to use this feature.

Ⓖ Categories

This area displays the iTunes Library categories that you can view.

Ⓕ Contents

The contents of the current iTunes Library source appear here.

Play a Song

You use the Music category of the iTunes Library to play a song that is stored on your computer. Although iTunes offers several methods to locate the song you want to play, the easiest method is to display the albums you have in your iTunes Library, and then open the album that contains the song you want to play.

While the song is playing, you can control the volume to suit the music or your current location. If you need to leave the room or take a call, you can pause the song currently playing.

Play a Song

1 Click **Music**.

2 Click **Albums**.

3 Double-click the album that contains the song you want to play.

A If you want to play the entire album, click **Play Album**.

4 Click the song you want to play.

5 Click the **Play** button ().

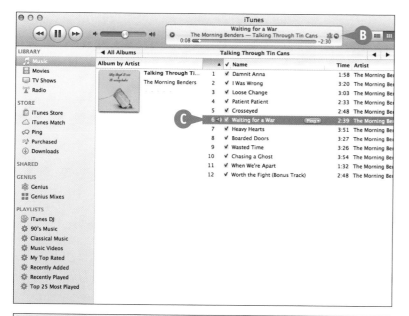

iTunes begins playing the song.

Ⓑ Information about the song playback appears here.

Ⓒ iTunes displays a speaker icon (🔊) beside the currently playing song.

Ⓓ If you need to stop the song temporarily, click the **Pause** button (⏸).

Note: *You can also pause and restart a song by pressing the* [Spacebar].

Ⓔ You can use the Volume slider to adjust the volume (see the Tip).

Note: *See the "Play a Music CD" section to learn more about the playback buttons.*

simplify it

How do I adjust the volume?
To turn the volume up or down, click and drag the **Volume** slider to the left (to reduce the volume) or to the right (to increase the volume). You can also press ⌘+⬇ to reduce the volume, or ⌘+⬆ to increase the volume. To mute the volume, either drag the **Volume** slider all the way to the left, or press [Option]+⌘+⬇. To restore the volume, adjust the **Volume** slider or press [Option]+⌘+⬆.

Play a Music CD

You can play your favorite music CDs in iTunes. If your Mac has an optical drive (that is, a drive capable of reading CDs and DVDs), then you can insert an audio disc in the drive and the CD appears in the Devices section of the iTunes Library. When you click the CD, the iTunes contents area displays the individual tracks on the CD, and if you have an Internet connection, you see the name of each track as well as other track data. During playback, you can skip tracks, pause, and resume play.

Play a Music CD

Play a CD

① Insert a music CD into your Mac's optical drive.

Ⓐ The music CD appears in the iTunes Devices category.

iTunes asks if you want to import the CD.

② Click **No**.

Note: *To learn how to import a CD, see the section "Import Tracks from a Music CD."*

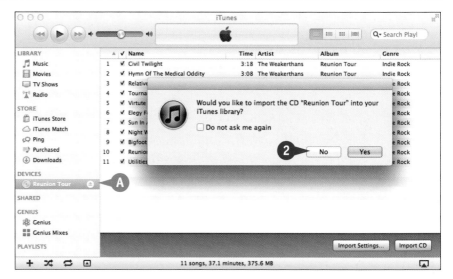

Ⓑ If you have an Internet connection, iTunes shows the contents of the CD.

Note: *iTunes shows the contents for most CDs, but it may not show the correct information for some discs, particularly noncommercial mixed CDs.*

③ Click ▷.

iTunes begins playing the CD from the first track.

Skip a Track

1 Click the **Next** button (▶▶)
to skip to the next track.

Note: *You can also skip to
the next track by pressing*
⌘+→.

2 Click the **Previous** button
(◀◀) to skip to the
beginning of the current
track; click ◀◀ again to
skip to the previous track.

Note: *You can also skip to
the previous track by
pressing* ⌘+←.

Pause and Resume Play

1 Click ⏸ (⏸ changes
to ▶).

iTunes pauses playback.

2 Click ▶.

iTunes resumes playback
where you left off.

Can I change the CD's audio levels?
Yes, iTunes has a graphic equalizer component
that you can use to adjust the levels. To
display the equalizer, click **Window** and then
click **Equalizer** (or press Option+⌘+2). In
the Equalizer window, use the sliders to set
the audio levels, or click the pop-up menu (⬚)
to choose an audio preset.

Can I display visualizations during playback?
Yes. You can click **View** and then click **Show
Visualizer** (you can also press ⌘+T). To
change the currently displayed visualizer,
click **View**, click **Visualizer**, and then click
the visualization you want to view.

continued

Play a Music
CD *(continued)*

iTunes gives you more options for controlling the CD playback. For example, you can easily switch from one song to another on the CD. You can also use the Repeat feature to tell iTunes to start the CD over from the beginning after it has finished playing the CD. iTunes also offers the Shuffle feature, which tells iTunes to play the CD's tracks in random order.

When the CD is done, you can use iTunes to eject it from your Mac. If you want to learn how to import music from the CD to iTunes, see the section *"Import Tracks from a Music CD."*

Play a Music CD *(continued)*

Play Another Song

① In the list of songs, double-click the song you want to play.

iTunes begins playing the song.

Repeat the CD

① Click the **Repeat** button (🔁 changes to 🔂).

iTunes restarts the CD after the last track finishes playing.

To repeat just the current song, click 🔁 again (🔁 changes to 🔂).

Play Songs Randomly

1 Click the **Shuffle** button (⤨ changes to ⤨).

iTunes shuffles the order of play.

Eject the CD

1 Click the **Eject** button (⏏) beside the CD.

Note: *You can also eject the CD by pressing and holding the ⏏ key on the keyboard.*

iTunes ejects the CD from your Mac's optical drive.

---

simplify it

Why do I not see the song titles after I insert my music CD?

When you play a music CD, iTunes tries to gather information about the album from the Internet. If you still see only track numbers, it may be that you do not have an Internet connection established or that you inserted a noncommercial mixed CD. Connect to the Internet, click **Advanced**, and then click **Get CD Track Names**.

Import Tracks from a Music CD

You can add tracks from a music CD to the iTunes Library. This enables you to listen to an album without having to put the CD into your Mac's optical drive each time. The process of adding tracks from a CD is called *importing,* or *ripping,* in OS X.

After you import the tracks from a music CD, you can play those tracks from the Music category of the iTunes Library. You can also use the tracks to create your own playlists and to create your own custom CDs.

Import Tracks from a Music CD

1 Insert a CD into your Mac's CD or DVD drive.

Ⓐ The music CD appears in the iTunes Devices category.

iTunes asks if you want to import the CD.

2 Click **No**.

Ⓑ If you want to import the entire CD, click **Yes** and skip the rest of the steps in this section.

Ⓒ iTunes shows the contents of the CD.

3 Click the check box so it is unchecked next to each CD track that you do not want to copy (☑ changes to ☐).

4 Click **Import CD**.

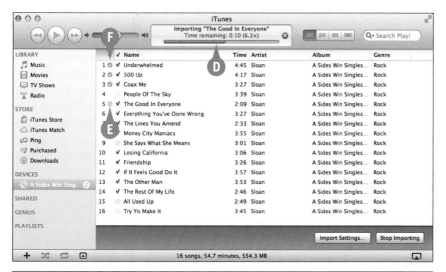

iTunes begins importing the check-marked track or tracks.

D This area displays the copy progress for each track.

E When iTunes is importing a track, it displays ⊚ beside the track number.

F When iTunes is finished importing a track, it displays ⊚ beside the track number.

G When iTunes has completed the import, you see ⊚ beside the track numbers of all the tracks you selected.

5 Click the **Eject** button (⏏) beside the CD, or press ⏏.

simplify it

I ripped a track by accident. How do I remove it from the Library?
Click the **Music** category, open the album you imported, right-click the track that you want to remove, and then click **Delete** from the shortcut menu. When iTunes asks you to confirm the deletion, click **Remove**. When iTunes asks if you want to keep the file, click **Move to Trash**.

Can I specify a different quality when importing?
Yes, by changing the *bit rate*, which is a measure of how much of the CD's original data is copied to your computer. Click **Import Settings** to open the Import Settings dialog. In the **Settings** pop-up menu, click ⬚, click **Custom**, and then use the Stereo Bit Rate pop-up to click the value you want.

Create a Playlist

A *playlist* is a collection of songs that are related in some way. Using your iTunes Library, you can create customized playlists that include only the songs that you want to hear.

For example, you might want to create a playlist of upbeat or festive songs to play during a party or celebration. Similarly, you might want to create a playlist of your current favorite songs to burn to a CD. Whatever the reason, once you create the playlist you can populate it with songs using a simple drag-and-drop technique.

Create a Playlist

Create the Playlist

1 Click **File**.

2 Click **New Playlist**.

> **Note:** *You can also choose the New Playlist command by pressing ⌘+N.*

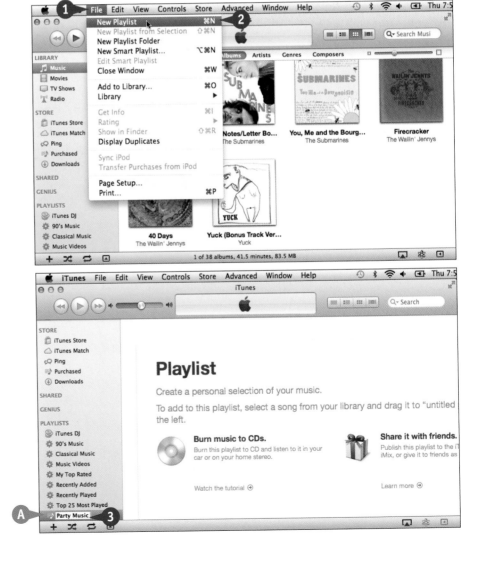

A iTunes creates a new playlist.

3 Type a name for the new playlist.

4 Press Return.

Add Songs to the Playlist

1 Click **Music**.

2 Open an album that has one or more songs you want to add to the playlist.

3 Click a song that you want to add to the playlist.

Note: *If you want more than one song from the album's playlist, hold down ⌘ and click each of the songs you want to add.*

4 Drag the selected track (or tracks) and drop them on your playlist.

5 Repeat Steps **2** to **4** to add more songs to the playlist.

6 Click the playlist.

B iTunes displays the songs you added to the playlist.

C If you want to listen to the playlist, click ▶.

---

simplify it

Is there any way to make iTunes add songs to a playlist automatically?
Yes, you can create a *smart playlist* where the songs that appear in the list have one or more properties in common, such as the genre, rating, artist, or text in the song title. Click **File** and then click **New Smart Playlist** (you can also press Option + ⌘ + N). Use the Smart Playlist dialog to create one or more rules that define which songs you want to appear in the playlist.

Burn Music Files to a CD

You can copy, or **burn**, music files from your Mac onto a CD. Burning CDs is a great way to create customized CDs that you can listen to on the computer or on any device that plays CDs.

You can burn music files from within the iTunes window. The easiest way to do this is to create a playlist of the songs you want to burn to the CD. You then organize the playlist by sorting the tracks in the order you want to hear them. To burn music files to a CD, your Mac must have a recordable optical drive.

Burn Music Files to a CD

① Insert a blank CD into your Mac's recordable disc drive.

② If you already have iTunes running and your Mac asks you to choose an action, click **Ignore**.

Ⓐ If you do not yet have iTunes running, use the Action menu to click ⬍, click **Open iTunes**, and then click **OK**.

③ Create a playlist for the songs you want to burn to the disc.

Note: *See the section "Create a Playlist" to learn how to build an iTunes playlist.*

④ Click the playlist that you want to burn.

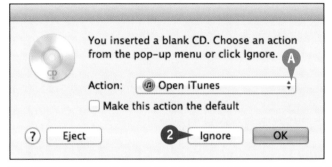

5 To modify the play order, click and drag a song and drop it on a new position in the playlist.

6 Repeat Step **5** to get the songs in the order in which you want them to appear on the CD.

7 Click **File**.

8 Click **Burn Playlist to Disc**.

The Burn Settings dialog appears.

9 Click **Burn**.

iTunes burns the songs to the CD.

simplify it

Can I control the interval between songs on the CD?
Yes. By default, iTunes adds 2 seconds between each track on the CD. You can change that in the Burn Settings dialog. In the Gap Between Songs pop-up menu, click ⬦, and then click the interval you want to use: None, or any time between 1 second and 5 seconds.

What happens if I have more music than can fit on a single disc?
You can still add all the music you want to burn to the playlist. iTunes fills the first disc and then adds the remaining songs to a second disc. After iTunes finishes burning the first disc, it prompts you to insert the next one.

Purchase Music from the iTunes Store

You can add music to your iTunes Library by purchasing songs or albums from the iTunes Store. iTunes downloads the song or album to your computer and then adds it to both the Music category and the Purchased playlist. You can then play and manage the song or album just like any other content in the iTunes Library.

To purchase music from the iTunes Store, you must have an Apple ID, which you can obtain from https://appleid.apple.com. You can also use an AOL account, if you have one.

Purchase Music from the iTunes Store

1 Click **iTunes Store**.

2 Click **Music**.

The iTunes Store appears.

3 Locate the music you want to purchase.

Ⓐ You can use the Search box to search for an artist, album, or song.

4 Click **Buy Album**.

Ⓑ If you want to purchase just a song, click the song's **Buy** button instead.

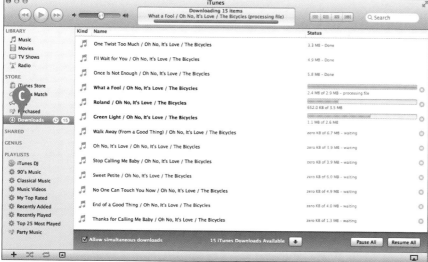

iTunes asks you to sign in to your iTunes Store account.

5 If you have not signed in to your account, you must type your Apple ID.

6 Type your password.

7 Click **Buy**.

iTunes charges your credit card and begins downloading the music to your Mac.

C To watch the progress of the download, click **Downloads**.

---

simplify it

Can I use my purchased music on other computers and devices?
Yes. Although many iTunes Store media, particularly movies and TV shows, have digital rights management (DRM) restrictions applied to prevent illegal copying, music in the iTunes Store is DRM-free. You can play songs on multiple computers and media devices, such as iPods, iPads, and iPhones, and burn them to multiple CDs.

How do I avoid having many $0.99 charges on my credit card bill when purchasing multiple songs?
To avoid many small iTunes charges, purchase an iTunes gift card. On the back of the card, scratch off the sticker that covers the redeem code. In iTunes, access the iTunes Store and click **Redeem** at the bottom of the store. Type in the redeem code and then click **Redeem**.

CHAPTER 9

Learning Useful OS X Tasks

OS X Mountain Lion comes with many tools that help you accomplish everyday tasks. In this chapter you learn how to connect and synchronize an iPod, iPhone, or iPad; work with notes and reminders; post to Twitter; share data; and work with notifications.

Connect an iPod, iPhone, or iPad

Before you can synchronize data between OS X and your iPod, iPhone, or iPad, you need to connect the device to your Mac. To connect an iPod, iPhone, or iPad, you need the USB cable that came as part of the device package. You will connect one end of that cable to your Mac, so you need to make sure that your Mac has a free USB port for the connection. You can also connect an iPod, iPhone, or iPad using an optional dock.

Connect an iPod, iPhone, or iPad

Connect the iPod, iPhone, or iPad

1 Using the device cable, attach the USB connector to a free USB port on your Mac.

2 Attach the other end of the cable to the port on the device or dock.

Mac OS X launches iTunes and automatically begins synchronizing the device.

Note: *Mac OS X usually also launches iPhoto to synchronize photos from the iPhone, iPad, or iPod touch. Either quit iPhoto or switch to iTunes.*

Disconnect the iPod, iPhone, or iPad

1 In iTunes, click the **eject** button (⏏) beside your device's name.

iTunes begins releasing the device.

Note: *See the tips section to learn when it is safe to disconnect the cable from an iPod.*

2 Pinch the sides of the connector and then pull the connector away from the device.

3 Disconnect the cable from the Mac's USB port.

Note: *If your Mac has two or more free USB ports and you synchronize your device frequently, consider leaving the cable plugged into a USB port for easier connections in the future.*

---

simplify it

Is there a way to prevent iTunes from starting the synchronization automatically when I connect my device?
Yes. In iTunes, click **iTunes** and then click **Preferences** to open the iTunes preferences window. Click the **Devices** tab and then click the **Prevent iPods, iPhones, and iPads from syncing automatically** check box (☐ changes to ☑). Click **OK.**

Do I have to use the USB cable to sync my device?
No. Connect your device as described in this section, click the Summary tab, and then click the **Sync with the** *device* **over Wi-Fi** option, where *device* is iPhone, iPad, or iPod (☐ changes to ☑). To sync over Wi-Fi, on your device tap **Settings**, tap **General**, tap **iTunes Wi-Fi Sync**, and then tap **Sync Now.**

Synchronize an iPod, iPhone, or iPad

You can take your media and other data with you by synchronizing that data from OS X to your device. For media, you can synchronize the music, movies, and TV shows in your iTunes library, as well as the photos in your iPhoto library, to your iPod, iPhone, or iPad.

However, you should synchronize movies and TV shows with care. A single half-hour TV episode may be as large as 650MB, and full-length movies can be several gigabytes, so even a modest video collection will consume a lot of storage space on your device.

Synchronize an iPod, iPhone, or iPad

Synchronize Music

1 Click your device.

2 Click **Music**.

3 Click **Sync Music**.

4 Click **Selected playlists, artists, albums, and genres**.

5 Click the check box beside each item you want to synchronize.

6 Click **Apply** to synchronize your music.

Synchronize Photos

1 Click your device.

2 Click **Photos**.

3 Click **Sync Photos from**.

4 Click **Selected albums, events, and faces, and automatically include**.

5 Click the check box beside each item you want to synchronize.

6 Click **Apply**.

iTunes synchronizes your photos.

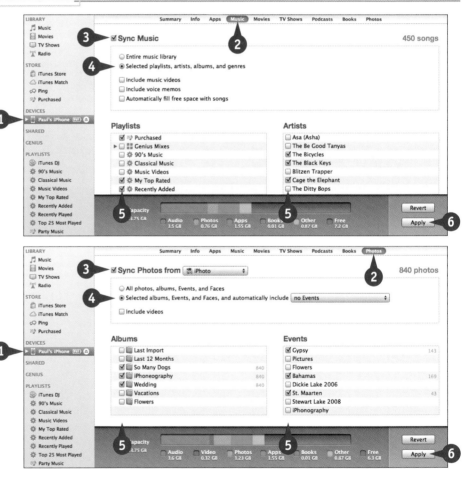

Synchronize Movies

1 Click your device.

2 Click **Movies**.

3 Click **Sync Movies**
(☐ changes to ☑).

4 Click each movie you
want to synchronize
(☐ changes to ☑).

5 Click **Apply**.

iTunes synchronizes
your movies.

Synchronize TV Shows

1 Click your device.

2 Click **TV Shows**.

3 Click **Sync TV Shows**
(☐ changes to ☑).

4 Click each TV
show you want
to synchronize
(☐ changes to ☑).

5 Click **Apply**.

iTunes synchronizes
your TV shows.

---

simplify it

Is there a way to control which music is synchronized to my iPod Shuffle?
Yes. You can configure iTunes to send a playlist instead. Connect your iPod Shuffle, click it in the Devices section, and then click the **Contents** tab. Click the **Autofill From** ⬚, click the playlist you want to send to the device, and then click **Autofill**.

How do I get my photos from my device to my Mac?
You can view and work with your camera pictures on your Mac by importing them to iPhoto. In iPhoto, click your device, then press and hold ⌘ and click each photo you want to import. Use the Event Name text box to type a name for this event, and then click **Import Selected**.

continued

Synchronize an iPod, iPhone, or iPad *(continued)*

If you will be away from your Mac, you can stay in touch by synchronizing your contacts, calendars, and e-mail accounts. The iPod touch, iPhone, and iPad include contacts, calendar, and e-mail tools, so you can ensure you are always dealing with the same data by synchronizing your Mac's contacts, calendars, and e-mail accounts to your device.

If you have an iPod touch, iPhone, or iPad, you can download apps from the App Store. You can do this using the App Store on the device, but you can also download apps using OS X and then synchronize the apps to your device.

Synchronize an iPod, iPhone, or iPad *(continued)*

Synchronize Contacts

1 Click your device.

2 Click **Info**.

3 Click **Sync Contacts**
(☐ changes to ☑).

4 Click **All contacts**
(☐ changes to ⦿).

5 Click **Apply**.

iTunes synchronizes your contacts.

Synchronize Calendars

1 Click your device.

2 Click **Info**.

3 Click **Sync Calendars**
(☐ changes to ☑).

4 Click **All calendars**
(☐ changes to ⦿).

5 Click **Apply**.

iTunes synchronizes your calendars.

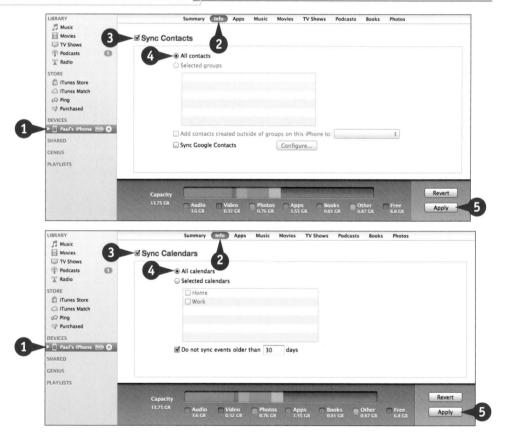

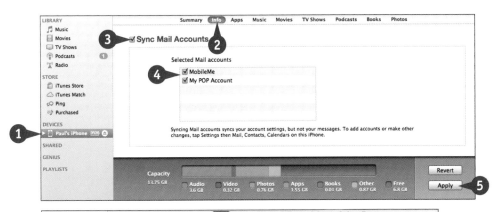

Synchronize E-mail Accounts

1 Click your device.

2 Click **Info**.

3 Click **Sync Mail Accounts** (☐ changes to ☑).

4 Click the check box beside each account you want to synchronize.

5 Click **Apply**.

iTunes synchronizes your selected e-mail accounts.

Synchronize Apps

1 Click your device in the iTunes Devices list.

2 Click **Apps**.

3 Click **Sync Apps** (☐ changes to ☑).

4 Click the check box beside each app you want to synchronize.

5 Click **Apply**.

iTunes synchronizes your apps.

---

simplify it

Is there any other information I can synchronize with my iPhone or iPad?
Yes, you can also synchronize your bookmarks, which are your favorite websites that you have saved using the Safari web browser. In iTunes, click your device, click the **Info** tab, scroll down to the Other section, and then click the **Sync Safari bookmarks** check box (☐ changes to ☑).

Other

☑ Sync Safari bookmarks

Install a Program Using the App Store

You can enhance and extend Mac OS X by installing new programs from the App Store. Mac OS X comes with an impressive collection of applications — or *apps* — particularly if your Mac comes with the iLife suite preinstalled. However, Mac OS X does not offer a complete collection of apps. For example, Mac OS X lacks apps in categories such as productivity, personal finance, and business tools.

To fill in these gaps, you can use the App Store to locate, purchase, and install new programs, or look for apps that go beyond what the default Mac OS X programs can do.

Install a Program Using the App Store

1 In the Dock, click **App Store** ( ).

The App Store window appears.

2 Locate the app you want to install.

3 Click the price button.

Note: *If the app is free, click the Free button instead.*

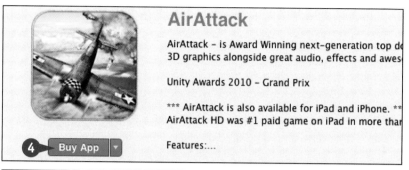

AirAttack

AirAttack – is Award Winning next-generation top do
3D graphics alongside great audio, effects and awes

Unity Awards 2010 – Grand Prix

*** AirAttack is also available for iPad and iPhone. **
AirAttack HD was #1 paid game on iPad in more thar

④ ━ Buy App ▼

Features:...

The price button changes to a
Buy App button, or the Free
button change to an Install
button.

④ Click **Buy App** (or **Install**).

Sign in to download from the App Store.
If you have an Apple ID, sign in with it here. If you have used the iTunes
Store or iCloud, for example, you have an Apple ID. If you don't have an
Apple ID, click Create Apple ID.

Apple ID
myaccount@me.com ◄ ⑤

Password   Forgot?
••••••••• ◄ ⑥

⑦ Cancel   Sign In ◄ ⑦

Create Apple ID

The App Store prompts you to
log in with your Apple ID.

⑤ Type your Apple ID.

⑥ Type your password.

⑦ Click **Sign In**.

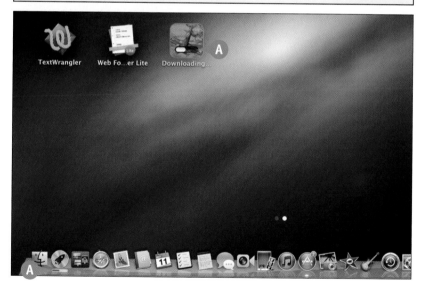

TextWrangler   Web Fo...er Lite   Downloading... Ⓐ

Ⓐ The App Store begins
downloading the app.

When the progress meter
disappears, your app is installed.
Click **Launchpad** (⬜) and then
click the app to run it.

**How do I use an App Store gift card to purchase
apps?**
Scratch off the sticker on the back to reveal the
code. Click ⬜ to open the App Store, click
Redeem Ⓐ, type the code, and then click
Redeem.

In the App Store window, the Account item Ⓑ
shows your current store credit balance.

Quick Links

Welcome Paul

Account $48.88 ◄ Ⓑ

Ⓐ ► Redeem

Support

Write a Note

You can use the Notes app to create simple text documents for things such as to-do lists and meeting notes. Word processing programs such as Word and Pages are useful for creating complex and lengthy documents. However, these powerful tools feel like overkill when all you want to do is jot down a few notes. For these simpler text tasks, the Notes app that comes with OS X Mountain Lion is perfect because it offers a simple interface that keeps all your notes together. As you see in the next section, you can also pin a note to the OS X desktop for easy access.

Write a Note

Create a New Note

1 In the Dock, click **Notes (▣)**.

The Notes window appears.

2 Click **New Note (⊞)**.

Note: *You can also click **File** and then click **New Note**, or press ⌘+Ⓝ.*

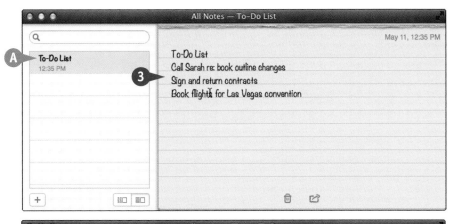

A The Notes app creates the new note.

③ Type your note text.

Delete a Note

① Click the note you want to delete.

② Click **Delete selected notes** (🗑).

The Notes app deletes the note.

How do I create a bulleted or numbered list?
Position the cursor where you want the list to begin, click **Format**, and then click **Lists**. In the menu that appears, click Insert Bulleted List, Insert Dashed List, or Insert Numbered List.

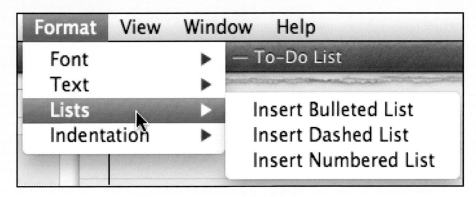

Pin a Note to the Desktop

You can ensure that you always see the content of a note by pinning that note to the OS X desktop. The Notes app is useful for setting up to-do lists, jotting down things to remember, and creating similar documents that contain text that you need to refer to while you work. Rather than constantly switching back and forth between Notes and your working application, you can pin a note to the desktop, which forces the note to stay visible, even when you switch to another application.

Pin a Note to the Desktop

1 Double-click the note you want to pin.

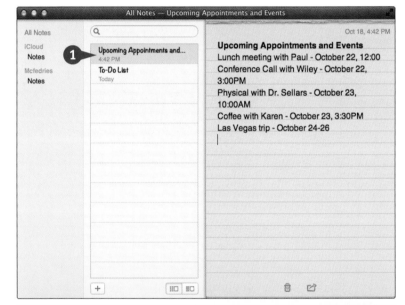

The Notes app opens the note in its own window.

2 Click and drag the note title to the position you want.

3 Click **Window**.

4 Click **Float on Top**.

A The Notes app keeps each opened note on top of any other window you open.

Am I only able to pin one note at a time to the desktop?
No, the Notes app enables you to pin multiple notes to the OS X desktop. This is useful if you have different notes that apply to the same task that you are working on in another application. However, you need to exercise some caution as the pinned notes take up space on the desktop, so you need to leave enough room to work in your other applications.

Create a Reminder

You can use the Reminders app to have OS X display a notification when you need to perform a task. You can use the Calendar app to schedule important events, but you likely have many tasks during the day that cannot be considered full-fledged events: returning a call, taking clothes out of the dryer, turning off the sprinkler. If you need to be reminded to perform such tasks, the Calendar app is overkill, but OS X offers a better solution: the Reminders app. You use this app to create reminders, which are notifications that tell you to do something or to be somewhere.

Create a Reminder

1 In the Dock, click
Reminders (□).

The Reminders app appears.

2 Click **New Reminder** (⊞).

Ⓐ You can also click the next available line in the Reminders list.

Note: *You can also click **File** and then click **New Reminder**, or press ⌘+N.*

③ Type the reminder title.

④ Click the **Show Info** icon (▣).

The Reminders app displays the reminder details.

⑤ Click **On a Day** (☐ changes to ☑).

⑥ Specify the date and time you want to be reminded.

⑦ Click **Done**.

The Reminders app adds the reminder to the list.

Ⓑ When you have completed the reminder, click its check box (☐ changes to ☑).

What does the At a Location option do?
It enables Reminders to display a notification when you arrive at or leave a location with your Mac notebook. To set this up, follow Steps **1** to **4**, click **At a Location** (☐ changes to ☑), then type the address or choose a contact that has a defined address. Click either **Leaving** or **Arriving** (☐ changes to ◉), and then click **Done**.

Create a New Reminder List

You can organize your reminders and make them easier to locate by creating new reminder lists. By default, the Reminders app comes with a single list called Reminders. However, if you use reminders frequently, the Reminders list can become cluttered, making it difficult to locate reminders. To solve this problem, you can organize your reminders by creating new lists. For example, you could have one list for personal tasks and another for business tasks. After you have created one or more new lists, you can move some or all of your existing reminders to the appropriate lists.

Create a New Reminder List

Create a Reminder List

1 Click **New List** (⊞).

> **Note:** *You can also click **File** and then click **New List**, or press ⌘+L.*

A The Reminders app adds the new list to the sidebar.

2 Type the list name.

3 Press Return.

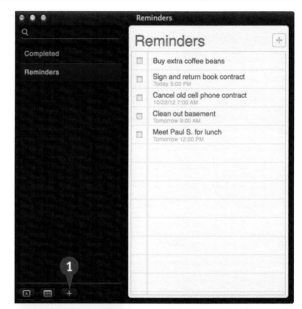

Move a Reminder to a Different List

1 Click the list that contains the reminder you want to move.

2 Click and drag the reminder and drop it on the destination list.

3 Click the destination list.

B The reminder now appears in the destination list.

Note: *You can also right-click the reminder, click Move to List, and then click the destination list.*

Why does my Reminders app not have a Completed list?
The Reminders app does not show the Completed list when you first start using the program. When you mark a reminder as complete by clicking its check box (☐ changes to ☑), Reminders creates the Completed list and moves the task to that list.

Can I change the order of the lists in the sidebar?
Yes. You might find it easier to work with several lists if they are in, say, alphabetical order. To move a list to a new position, click and drag the list up or down in the sidebar. When the horizontal blue bar shows the list to be in the position you want, release the mouse button.

Sign In to Your Twitter Account

If you have a Twitter account, you can use it to share information with your followers directly from OS X Mountain Lion. OS X Mountain Lion comes with built-in support for Twitter. This enables you to send tweets directly from many OS X apps. For example, you can send a link to a web page from Safari or

tweet a photo from Photo Booth. OS X also displays notifications if you are mentioned on Twitter or if a Twitter user sends you a direct message. Before you can tweet or see Twitter notifications, you must sign in to your Twitter account.

Sign In to Your Twitter Account

1 Click **System Preferences** ( ).

Note: *You can also click the Apple icon ( ) and then click* ***System Preferences***.

The System Preferences window appears.

2 Click **Mail, Contacts & Calendars**.

The Mail, Contacts & Calendars window appears.

③ Click the Twitter logo.

System Preferences prompts you for your Twitter username and password.

④ Type your Twitter username.

⑤ Type your Twitter password.

⑥ Click **Sign In**.

OS X signs in to your Twitter account.

Some of the people in my contacts list are on Twitter. Is there an easy way to add their Twitter usernames to the Contacts app?

Yes, OS X Mountain Lion has a feature that enables you to update Contacts with Twitter usernames and account photos.

Follow Steps **1** and **2** to open the Mail, Contacts & Calendars window, click your Twitter account, and then click **Update Contacts**. When OS X asks you to confirm, click **Update Contacts**.

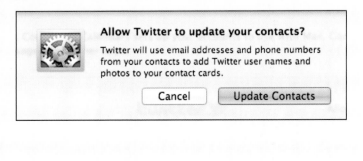

Send a Tweet

After you sign in to your Twitter account in OS X Mountain Lion, you can send tweets from various OS X apps. Although signing in to your Twitter account is useful for seeing notifications that tell you about mentions and direct messages, you will mostly use it for sending tweets to your followers. For example, if you come across a web page that you want to share, you can tweet a link to that page. You can also take a picture using Photo Booth and tweet that picture to your followers.

Send a Tweet

Tweet a Web Page

1 Use Safari to navigate to the web page you want to share.

2 Click **Share** (⬆).

3 Click **Twitter**.

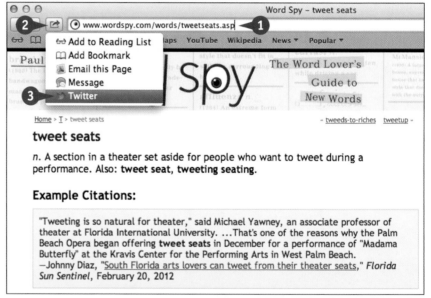

OS X displays the Twitter share sheet.

Ⓐ The attachment appears as a link inside the tweet.

4 Type your tweet text.

Ⓑ This value tells you how many characters you have remaining.

5 Click **Send**.

Learning Useful OS X Tasks

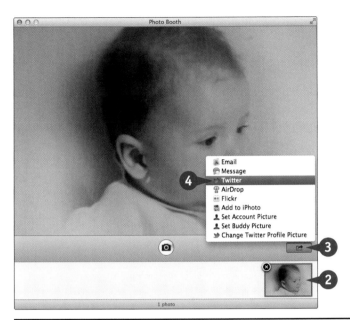

Tweet a Photo Booth Photo

1 Use Photo Booth to take a picture.

2 Click the picture you want to share.

3 Click **Share** (⬆).

4 Click **Twitter**.

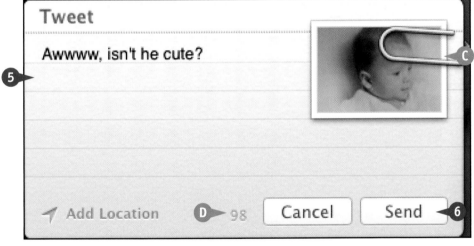

OS X displays the Twitter share sheet.

C The attachment appears as a link inside the tweet.

5 Type your tweet text.

D This value tells you how many characters you have remaining.

6 Click **Send**.

---

simplify it

Are there other apps I can use to send tweets?

Yes. If you open a photo using Quick Look (click the photo in Finder and then press Spacebar), you can click **Share** (⬆) and then click **Twitter**. Similarly, you can open a photo in Preview, click ⬆ and then click **Twitter**.

Share Information with Other People

You can use OS X Mountain Lion to share information with other people, including web pages, notes, pictures, videos, and photos. OS X Mountain Lion was built with sharing in mind. In previous versions of OS X, it was often difficult or tedious to share

information such as web pages, images, and videos. OS X Mountain Lion implements a feature called the *share sheet*, which makes it easy to share data using multiple methods, such as e-mail, instant messaging, and Twitter.

Share Information with Other People

Share a Web Page

1. Use Safari to navigate to the web page you want to share.

2. Click **Share** (⬆).

3. Click the method you want to use to share the web page.

Share a Note

1. In the Notes app, click the note you want to share.

2. Click **Share** (⬆).

3. Click the method you want to use to share the note.

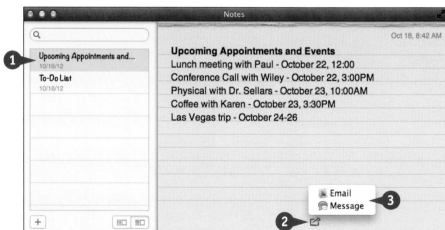

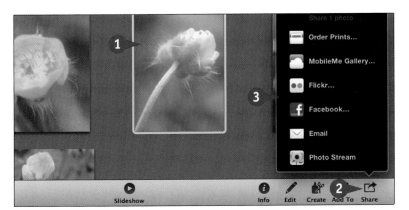

Share a Picture

1 In iPhoto, click the picture you want to share.

2 Click **Share** (📤).

3 Click the method you want to use to share the picture.

Share a Video

1 In QuickTime Player, open the video you want to share.

2 Click **Share** (📤).

3 Click the method you want to use to share the video.

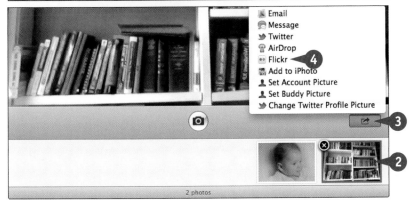

Share a Photo

1 Use Photo Booth to snap a photo.

2 Click the photo.

3 Click **Share** (📤).

4 Click the method you want to use to share the photo.

Do I need to configure OS X to use some of the sharing methods?

Yes, in most cases. For example, you cannot use the Email method unless you configure Mail with an e-mail account, and you cannot use the Message method until you configure Messages with an account. Other services such as Flickr and Vimeo must be configured in System Preferences.

Work with the Notification Center

You can keep on top of what is happening while you are using your Mac by taking advantage of the Notification Center. Several OS X Mountain Lion apps take advantage of a feature called notifications, which enables them to send messages to OS X about events and alerts that are happening on your Mac. For example, the App Store uses the Notification Center to let you know when there are OS X updates available. There are two types of notifications: a banner that appears on the desktop temporarily, and an alert that stays on the desktop until you dismiss it. You can also open the Notification Center to view your recent notifications.

Work with the Notification Center

Handle Alert Notifications

A An alert notification displays one or more buttons.

1 Click a button to dismiss the notification.

B In a notification about new OS X updates, click **Update** to open the App Store and see the updates.

C For details about the updates, click **Details**.

Handle Banner Notifications

D A banner notification does not display any buttons.

Note: *The banner notification stays onscreen for about five seconds and then disappears.*

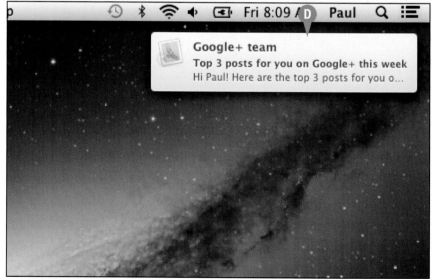

View Recent Notifications

1 Click **Notification Center** (☰).

Note: *If your Mac has a trackpad, you can also open the Notification Center by using two fingers to swipe left from the right edge of the trackpad.*

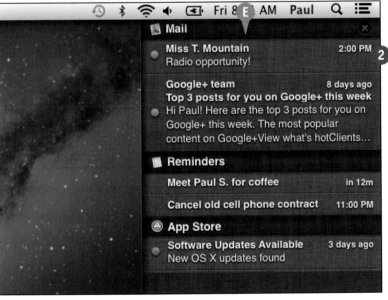

E OS X displays your recent notifications.

2 Click a notification to view the item in the original application.

Can I control which apps use the Notification Center and how they use it?
Yes. Click **System Preferences** (⚙) in the Dock and then click **Notifications**. Click an app on the left side of the window, and then click a notification style: Alerts, Banners, or None. To control the maximum number of items the app can display in the Notification Center, click the **Show in Notification Center** pop-up and then click a number. To remove an app from the Notification Center, click the **Show in Notification Center** check box (☑ changes to ☐).

Connect to a Wireless Network

If your Mac has built-in wireless networking capabilities, you can use them to connect to a wireless network that is within range. This could be a network in your home, your office, or a public location such as a coffee shop. In most cases, this will also give you access to the wireless network's Internet connection.

Most wireless networks have security turned on, which means you must know the correct password to connect to the network. However, after you have connected to the network once, your Mac remembers the password, and will connect again automatically the next time the network comes within range.

Connect to a Wireless Network

1 Click the **Wi-Fi status** icon (📶) in the menu bar.

Your Mac locates the wireless networks within range of your Mac.

Ⓐ The available networks appear in the menu.

Ⓑ Networks with a Lock icon (🔒) require a password to join.

2 Click the wireless network you want to join.

The Wi-Fi network "Galt Ave" requires a WPA password.

Password: •••••••••• — **3**

C — ☐ Show password
☑ Remember this network

(?)   Cancel   Join — **4**

If the wireless network is secure, your Mac prompts you for the password.

3 Use the Password text box to type the network password.

C If the password is very long and you are sure no one can see your screen, you can click **Show password** (☐ changes to ☑) to see the actual characters instead of dots. This helps to ensure you type the password correctly.

4 Click **Join**.

Your Mac connects to the wireless network.

D The Wi-Fi status icon changes from 🛜 to 🛜 to indicate the connection.

I know a particular network is within range, but I do not see it in the list. Why not?
As a security precaution, some wireless networks do not broadcast their availability. To connect to such a network, click 🛜 and then click **Join Other Network**. Type the name of the network, click the **Security** ⬦, click the network's security type, then follow steps **3** and **4** to join the network.

I do not see the Wi-Fi status icon on my menu bar. How do I display the icon?
You can do this using System Preferences. Click the System Preferences icon (🎛) in the Dock (or click and then click **System Preferences**) to open the System Preferences window. Click **Network**, click **Wi-Fi**, and then click the **Show Wi-Fi status in menu bar** check box (☐ changes to ☑).

CHAPTER 10

Viewing and Editing Photos

Whether you just want to look at your photos, or you want to edit them to crop out unneeded portions or fix problems, OS X comes with a number of useful tools for this purpose.

View a Preview
of a Photo

OS X offers several tools you can use to see a preview of any photo on your Mac. The Finder application has a number of methods you can use to view your photos, but here you learn about the two easiest methods. First, you can preview any saved image file using the OS X Quick Look feature; second, you can see photo previews by switching to the Cover Flow view. You can also preview photos using the Preview application.

View a Preview of a Photo

View a Preview with Quick Look

1 Click **Finder** (📷) in the Dock.

2 Open the folder that contains the photo you want to preview.

3 Click the photo.

4 Click **Quick Look** (👁).

You can also right-click the photo and then click **Quick Look**, or press `Spacebar`.

Ⓐ Finder displays a preview of the photo.

View a Preview with Cover Flow

1 Click **Finder** (📷) in the Dock.

2 Open the folder that contains the photo you want to preview.

3 Click the photo.

4 Click **Cover Flow** (▦).

Ⓑ Finder displays a preview of the photo.

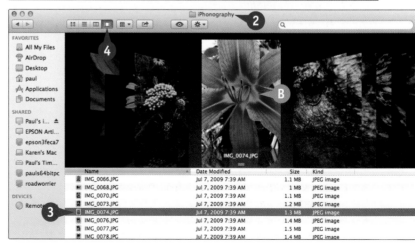

View a Preview in the Preview Application

1 Click **Finder** (🖥) in the Dock.

2 Open the folder that contains the photo you want to preview.

3 Click the photo.

4 Click **File**.

5 Click **Open With**.

6 Click **Preview**.

Note: *In many cases, you can also simply double-click the photo to open it in the Preview application.*

The Preview application opens and displays the photo.

7 Use the toolbar buttons to change how the photo appears in the Preview window.

C More commands are available on the **View** menu.

8 When you are finished viewing the photo, click **Close** (⊙).

Is there an easier way to preview multiple photos using the Preview application?
Yes. In Finder, navigate to the folder that contains the photos, and then select each file that you want to preview. Either click and drag the mouse ▶ over the photos or press and hold ⌘ and click each one. In Preview, click **Next** and **Previous** to navigate the photos.

Is there a way that I can zoom in on just a portion of a photo?
Yes. In Preview, click **Tools** and then click **Select Tool** (or either press ⌘+3 or click **Select** in the toolbar). Click and drag your mouse ▶ to select the portion of the photo that you want to magnify. Click **View** and then click **Zoom to Selection** (or press ⌘+*).

View a Slide Show
of Your Photos

Instead of viewing your photos one at a time, you can easily view multiple photos by running them in a slide show. You can run the slide show using the Preview application. The slide show displays each photo for a few seconds, and then Preview

automatically displays the next photo. Quick Look also offers several on-screen controls that you can use to control the slide show playback. You can also configure Quick Look to display the images full-screen.

View a Slide Show of Your Photos

1 Click **Finder** (🖥️) in the Dock.

2 Open the folder that contains the photos you want to view in the slide show.

3 Select the photos you want to view.

4 Click **File**.

5 Click **Open With**.

6 Click **Preview**.

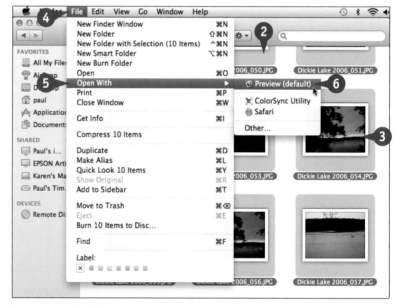

The Preview window appears.

7 Click **View**.

8 Click **Slideshow**.

You can also select Slideshow by pressing Shift + ⌘ + F.

Preview opens the slide show window.

9 Move the mouse ➤.

A Preview displays the slide show controls.

10 Click **Play**.

Preview begins the slide show.

B Click **Next** to move to the next photo.

C Click **Back** to move to the previous photo.

D Click **Pause** to suspend the slide show.

11 When the slide show is over or when you want to return to Finder, click **Close** or press Esc.

Can I jump to a specific photo during the slide show?
Yes. With the slide show running, press Return to stop the show. Use the arrow keys to select the photo that you want to view in the slide show, and then press Return. Preview returns you to the slide show and displays the selected photo. Click **Play** to resume the slide show.

What keyboard shortcuts can I use when viewing a slide show?
Press → or ↑ to display the next photo, and press ← or ↓ to display the previous photo. Press Esc to end the slide show.

Open and Close iPhoto

Your Mac has iLife installed, and the suite includes the iPhoto application, which offers special tools for viewing, managing, and editing your photos. You can also purchase iPhoto separately through the App Store. With iPhoto you can import photos from a digital camera, view and organize the photos on your Mac, and edit and repair photos.

To begin using the program, you must first learn how to find and open the iPhoto window. When you finish using the program, you can close the iPhoto window to free up computer processing power.

Open and Close iPhoto

Open iPhoto

1 In the Dock, click **iPhoto** (📷).

The iPhoto window appears.

The first time you launch iPhoto, the program asks if you want to use iPhoto when you connect your digital camera.

2 Click **Yes**.

The first time you launch iPhoto, the program asks if you want to view your photos on a map.

3 If you have a GPS-enabled camera (such as an iPhone 3G or later, or an iPad 2 or later with 3G or 4G) or if you want to enter location data manually, click **Yes**.

Close iPhoto

① Click **iPhoto**.

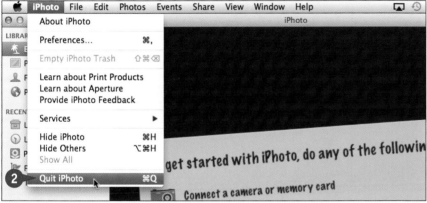

② Click **Quit iPhoto**.

Are there other methods I can use to open iPhoto?

Yes. If you do not have 🖼 in the Dock, there are a couple of methods you can use to open iPhoto. If you have used iPhoto recently, a reasonably fast method is to click the Apple icon (🍎), click **Recent Items**, and then click **iPhoto**. Alternatively, click **Spotlight** (🔍), type **iphoto**, and then click **iPhoto** in the search results.

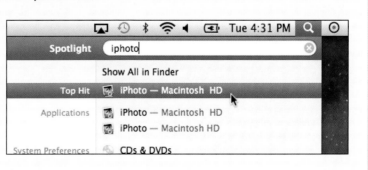

Import Photos from a Digital Camera

You can import photos from a digital camera and save them on your Mac. If you have the iLife suite installed on your Mac, you can use the iPhoto application to handle importing photos.

iPhoto is also available separately through the App Store. iPhoto enables you to add a name and a

description to each import, which helps you to find your photos after the import is complete. To perform the import, you need a cable to connect your digital camera to your Mac. Most digital cameras come with a USB cable.

Import Photos from a Digital Camera

Import Photos from a Digital Camera

1 Connect one end of the cable to the digital camera.

2 Connect the other end of the cable to a free USB port on your Mac.

3 Turn the camera on and put it in either playback or computer mode.

Your Mac launches the iPhoto application.

A Your digital camera appears in the Devices section.

B iPhoto displays previews of the camera's photos.

4 In the Event Name text box, type a name for the group of photos you are going to import.

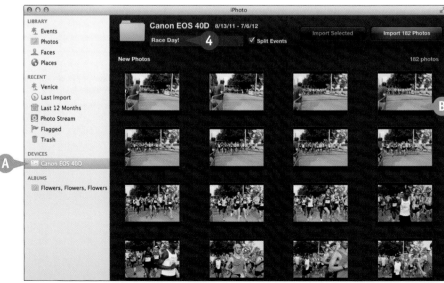

5 Click and drag the mouse ▸ around the photos you want to import, or press and hold ⌘ and click each photo.

6 Click **Import Selected**.

C To import all the photos from the digital camera, click **Import X Photos**, where X is the number of photos stored in the camera.

iPhoto imports the photos from the digital camera.

iPhoto asks if you want to delete the original photos from the digital camera.

7 If you no longer need the photos on the camera, click **Delete Photos**.

D To keep the photos on the camera, click **Keep Photos**.

View the Imported Photos

1 Click **Events**.

2 Double-click the event name that you specified in Step **4**.

simplify it

When I connect my digital camera, why do I see Image Capture instead of iPhoto?

You need to configure Image Capture to open iPhoto when you connect your camera by following these steps:

1 Connect your digital camera to your Mac.

The Image Capture application opens.

2 Click the **Connecting** ⬦ and then click **iPhoto**.

3 Click **Image Capture** in the menu bar.

4 Click **Quit Image Capture**.

View Your Photos

If you want to look at several photos, you can use the iPhoto application, which is available with the Apple iLife suite or separately via the App Store. iPhoto offers a feature called full-screen mode, which hides everything else and displays your photos using the entire screen. Once you activate full-screen mode, iPhoto offers several on-screen controls that you can use to navigate backward and forward through the photos in a folder. Full-screen mode also shows thumbnail images of each photo, so you can quickly jump to any photo you want to view.

View Your Photos

1 In iPhoto, click **Events**.

2 Double-click the event that contains the photos you want to view.

3 Double-click the first photo you want to view.

iPhoto displays the photo.

④ Click **Next** (▶) to view the next photo in the event.

Ⓐ You can also click **Previous** (◀) to see the previous photo in the event.

Note: *You can also navigate photos by pressing ▶ and ◀.*

⑤ When you are done, click the name of the event.

Is there a way that I can jump quickly to a particular photo in full-screen mode?
Yes. Follow these steps:

① Move the mouse ➤ to the thumbnails at the bottom of the iPhoto window.

② Use the horizontal scroll bar to bring the thumbnail of the photo you want into view.

③ Click the photo's thumbnail.

iPhoto displays the photo in full-screen mode.

Create an Album

You can use the iPhoto application to organize your photos into albums. You can get iPhoto either via the iLife suite, which is installed on all new Macs, or via the App Store. In iPhoto, an *album* is a collection of photos that are usually related in some way. For example, you might create an album for a series of vacation photos, for photos taken at a party or other special event, or for photos that include a particular person, pet, or place. Using your iPhoto Library, you can create customized albums that include only the photos that you want to view.

Create an Album

Create the Album

1 Click **File**.

2 Click **New Album**.

> **Note:** *You can also start a new album by pressing* ⌘+N.

iPhoto asks you to confirm that you want to create an empty album.

3 Click **Continue**.

4 Type a name for the new album.

5 Press Return.

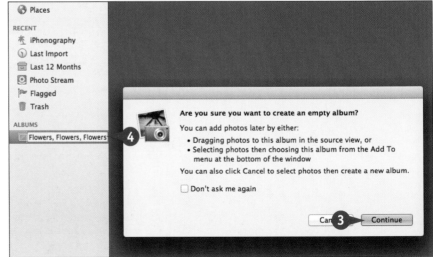

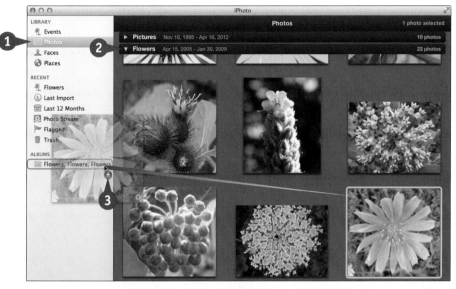

Add Photos to the Album

1 Click **Photos**.

2 Click ▶ beside an event that contains photos you want to work with (▶ changes to ▼).

3 Click and drag a photo and drop it on the new album.

4 Repeat Steps **2** and **3** to add other photos to the album.

5 Click the album.

A iPhoto displays the photos you added to the album.

Is there any way to make iPhoto add photos to an album automatically?
Yes, you can create a *smart album* where the photos that appear in the album have one or more properties in common. Click **File** and then click **New Smart Album**. Use the Smart Album dialog to create one or more rules that define which photos you want to appear in the album.

Smart Album name:	Favorites

Match the following condition:

| My Rating | ⬍ | is | ⬍ | ★★★★★ | ⊖ ⊕ |

Cancel   OK

Crop a Photo

If you have a photo containing elements that you do not want or need to see, you can often cut out those elements. This is called **cropping**, and you can do this with iPhoto, which comes with the iLife suite or via the App Store.

When you crop a photo, you specify a rectangular area of the photo that you want to keep. iPhoto

discards everything outside of the rectangle. Cropping is a useful skill to have because it can help give focus to the true subject of a photo. Cropping is also useful for removing extraneous elements that appear on or near the edges of a photo.

Crop a Photo

1 Click the photo you want to crop.

2 Click Edit (✏).

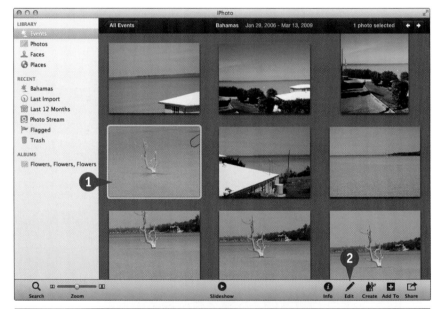

iPhoto displays its editing tools.

3 Click Crop (▣).

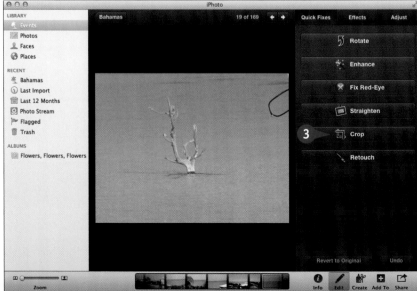

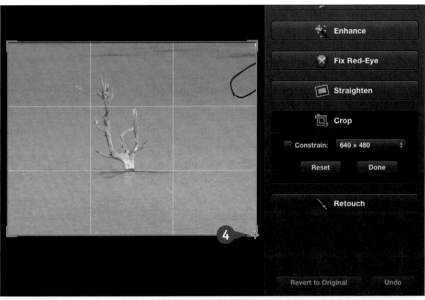

iPhoto displays a cropping rectangle on the photo.

④ Click and drag a corner or side to define the area you want to keep.

Note: *Remember that iPhoto keeps the area inside the rectangle.*

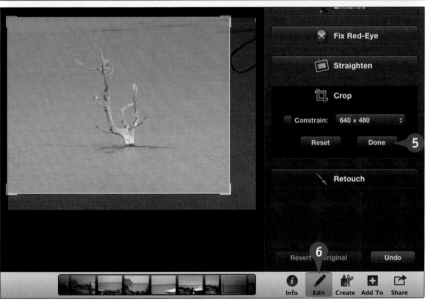

⑤ Click Done.

iPhoto saves the cropped photo.

⑥ Click Edit (![pencil]).

iPhoto exits edit mode.

Is there a quick way to crop a photo to a certain size?
Yes, iPhoto enables you to specify either a specific size, such as 640 x 480, or a specific ratio, such as 4 x 3 or 16 x 9.

① Follow Steps **1** to **3** to display the Crop tool.

② Click the Constrain check box (☐ changes to ☑).

③ In the Constrain pop-up menu, click ⬚.

④ Click the size or ratio you want to use.

⑤ Click Done.

⑥ Click ![pencil].

iPhoto exits edit mode.

Rotate a Photo

You can rotate a photo using the iPhoto application, which comes with all new Macs as part of iLife, and is also available separately via the App Store. Depending on how you held your camera when you took a shot, the resulting photo might show the subject sideways or upside down. This may be the effect you want, but more likely this is a problem. To fix this problem, you can use iPhoto to rotate the photo so that the subject appears right-side up. You can rotate a photo either clockwise or counterclockwise.

Rotate a Photo

① Click the photo you want to rotate.

Note: *A quick way to rotate a photo is to right-click the photo and then click **Rotate** (⬗).*

② Click Edit (✎).

iPhoto displays its editing tools.

③ Click Rotate (🔄).

Ⓐ iPhoto rotates the photo 90 degrees counterclockwise.

④ Repeat Step **3** until the subject of the photo is right-side up.

⑤ Click 🖊.

iPhoto exits edit mode.

Can I rotate a photo clockwise instead?
Yes, you can rotate a photo clockwise by following these steps:

① With the editing tools displayed, press and hold the Option key.

Ⓐ The Rotate icon changes from 🔄 to 🔃.

② Press and hold Option + click **Rotate** to rotate the photo clockwise by 90 degrees, or right-click the photo and then click **Rotate Clockwise**.

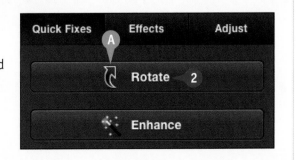

Straighten a Photo

You can straighten a crooked photo using the iPhoto application, which comes with all new Macs as part of iLife, and is also available separately via the App Store. If you do not use a tripod when taking pictures, getting your camera perfectly level when you take a shot is very difficult and requires a lot of practice and a steady hand. Despite your best efforts, you might end up with a photo that is not quite level. To fix this problem, you can use iPhoto to nudge the photo clockwise or counterclockwise so that the subject appears straight.

Straighten a Photo

1 Click the photo you want to straighten.

2 Click **Edit** (✎).

iPhoto displays its editing tools.

3 Click **Straighten** (▣).

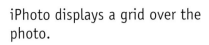

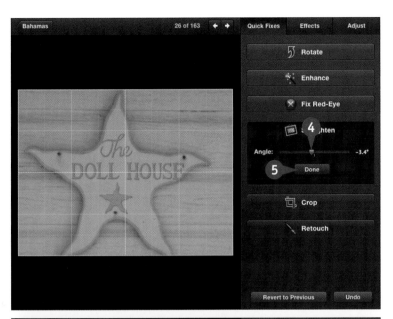

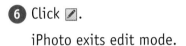

iPhoto displays a grid over the photo.

④ Click and drag the **Angle** slider.

Drag the slider to the left to angle the photo counterclockwise.

Drag the slider to the right to angle the photo clockwise.

⑤ Click **Done**.

⑥ Click 🖊.

iPhoto exits edit mode.

How do I know when my photo is level?
Use the gridlines that iPhoto places over the photo. Locate a horizontal line in your photo, and then rotate the photo so that this line is parallel to the nearest horizontal line in the grid. You can also match a vertical line in the photo with a vertical line in the grid.

Remove Red Eye from a Photo

You can remove red eye from a photo using the iPhoto application, which comes with all new Macs as part of iLife, and is also available separately via the App Store. When you use a flash to take a picture of one or more people, in some cases the flash may reflect off the subjects' retinas. The result is the common phenomenon of *red eye*, where each person's pupils appear red instead of black. If you have a photo where one or more people have red eyes due to the camera flash, you can use iPhoto to remove the red eye and give your subjects a more natural look.

Remove Red Eye from a Photo

1 Click the photo that contains the red eye.

2 Click **Edit** (◢).

iPhoto displays its editing tools.

Ⓐ If needed, you can click and drag this slider to the right to zoom in on the picture.

Ⓑ You can click and drag this rectangle to bring the red eye into view.

3 Click **Fix Red-Eye** (◉).

iPhoto displays its Red-Eye controls.

C You may be able to fix the red eye automatically by clicking the **Auto-fix red-eye** check box (☐ changes to ☑). If that does not work, continue with the rest of these steps.

4 Move the red eye pointer over a red eye in the photo.

5 Click the red eye.

D iPhoto removes the red eye.

6 Repeat Steps **4** and **5** to fix any other instances of red eye in the photo.

7 Click **Done**.

8 Click ✎.

iPhoto exits edit mode.

Why does iPhoto remove only part of the red eye in my photo?
The Red-Eye tool may not be set to a large enough size. The tool should be approximately the same size as the subject's eye:

1 Follow Steps **1** to **3** to display the Red-Eye controls.

2 Click and drag the Size slider until the Red-Eye tool is the size of the red-eye area.

3 Use your mouse to move the circle over the red eye and then click.

iPhoto removes the red eye that occurs within the circle.

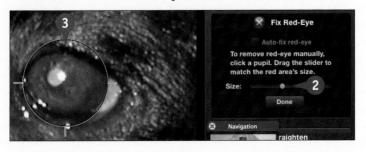

Add Names to Faces in Your Photos

You can make your photos easier to manage and navigate by adding names to the faces that appear in each photo. This is sometimes called *tagging*, and it enables you to navigate your photos by name. For example, you can view all your photos in which a certain person appears.

To add names to the faces in your photos, you must be using iPhoto '09 or later. To check this, click iPhoto in the menu bar and then click About iPhoto.

Add Names to Faces in Your Photos

① Click the photo that you want to tag.

② Click **Info** (ⓘ).

③ Click **X unnamed** (where *X* is the number of faces iPhoto identifies in the photo).

iPhoto displays its naming tools.

④ Click **unnamed**.

⑤ Type the person's name.

⑥ Press **Return**.

⑦ Repeat Steps **3** to **5** to name each person in the photo.

Ⓐ If iPhoto did not mark a face in the photo, click **Add a Face**, size and position the box over the face, and then type the name in the **click to name** box.

⑧ Click 🅘.

iPhoto exits naming mode.

How do I view all the photos that contain a particular person?

You can open a photo, click **Info** (🅘), and then click the **Show All** arrow (🔘) beside the person's name. You can also follow these steps:

① Click **Faces** in the iPhoto Sidebar.

Ⓐ iPhoto displays the names and sample photos of each person you have named.

② Double-click the person you want to view.

iPhoto displays all the photos that contain the person.

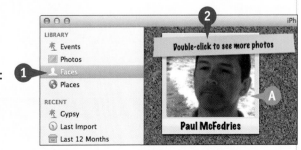

Map Your Photos

You can view your photos by location if you edit each photo to include the location where you took the image. If your camera does not add location data automatically, you can tell iPhoto the locations where your photos were taken, and then display a map that shows those locations. This enables you to view all your photos taken in a particular place.

To map your photos, you must be using iPhoto '09 or later. To check this, click iPhoto in the menu bar and then click About iPhoto.

Map Your Photos

① Click the event that you want to map.

If you want to map a single photo, open the event and then open the photo.

② Click **Info** (ⓘ).

③ Click **Assign a Place**.

④ Type the location.

Ⓐ iPhoto displays a list of locations that match what you typed.

⑤ When you see the place you want to use, click it.

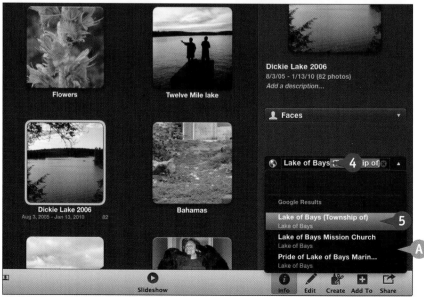

Viewing and Editing Photos

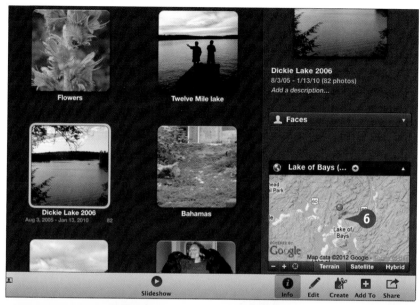

iPhoto displays the location on a Google map.

⑥ Click and drag the pin to the correct location, if necessary.

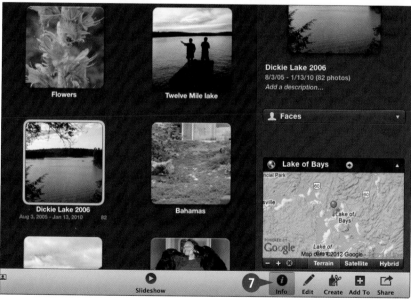

⑦ Click 🛈.

iPhoto closes the info window.

Is there a way to have the location data added automatically?

Yes. If you have a GPS-enabled camera, iPhoto automatically picks up location data from the photos; however, you must activate this feature. Click **iPhoto** in the menu bar, click **Preferences**, and then click the **Advanced** tab. Click the **Look up Places** ⊟ and then click **Automatically**. Note that you may still have to add or edit location names for your photos.

How do I view all the photos that were taken in a particular place?

Click **Places** in the iPhoto Sidebar to see a map of the world with pins for each of your photo locations. Position the mouse ⬈ over the location's pin, and then click the **Show All** arrow (⊙). iPhoto displays all the photos that were taken in that location.

E-mail a Photo

You can use the iPhoto application to create a message to send a photo to another person via e-mail. iPhoto comes with all new Macs as part of iLife, and is also available separately via the App Store.

If you have a photo that you want to share with someone, and you know that person's e-mail address, you can send the photo in an e-mail message. Using iPhoto, you can specify which photo you want to send, and iPhoto creates a new message. Even if a photo is very large, you can still send it via e-mail because you can use iPhoto to shrink the copy of the photo that appears in the message.

E-mail a Photo

1 Click the photo you want to send.

2 Click **Share**.

3 Click **Email**.

You can also click **Share** (📷) and then click **Email**.

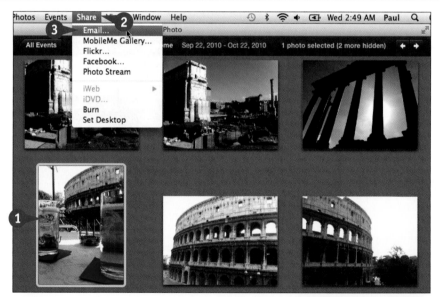

OS X asks if you want to set up iPhoto to e-mail photos.

Note: *This is a one-time setup task. In the future, you can skip directly to Step 7.*

4 Click **Setup**.

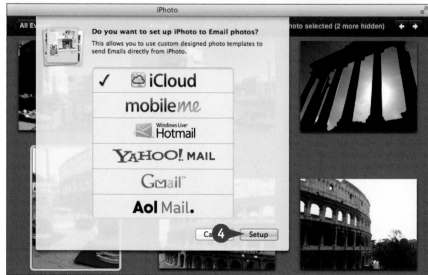

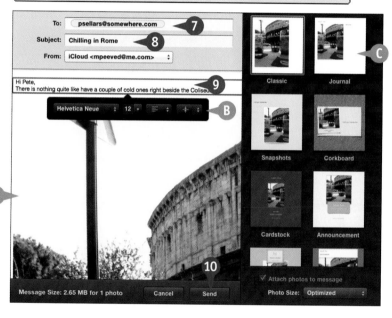

OS X displays the Add Account dialog.

5 Fill in the e-mail account details, which vary depending on the account type.

6 Click **Save**.

A iPhoto creates a new message and adds the photo to the message body.

7 Type the address of the message recipient.

8 Type the message subject.

9 Click here and then type your message text.

B You can use these controls to format the text.

C You can click these thumbnails to apply a special effect to the message.

10 Click **Send**.

iPhoto sends the message.

How do I change the size of the photo?
You need to be careful when sending photos because a single image can be several megabytes in size. If your recipient's e-mail system places restrictions on the size of messages it can receive, your message might not go through.

To change the size of the photo, click the **Photo Size** 🔅 and then click the size you want to use for the sent photo, such as Small or Medium. Note that this does not affect the size of the original photo, just the copy that is sent with the message.

Take Your Picture

You can use your Mac to take a picture of yourself. If your Mac comes with a built-in iSight or FaceTime HD camera, or if you have an external camera attached to your Mac, you can use the camera to take a picture of yourself using the Photo Booth application. After you have taken your picture, you can e-mail that picture, add it to iPhoto, or set it as your user account or iChat buddy picture.

Take Your Picture

Take Your Picture with Photo Booth

1 In the Dock, click **Photo Booth** (📷).

The Photo Booth window appears.

Ⓐ The live feed from the camera appears here.

2 Click **Take a still picture** (▢).

Ⓑ Click **Take four quick pictures** (▦) if you want Photo Booth to snap four successive photos, each about 1 second apart.

Ⓒ Click **Take a movie clip** (▣) if you want Photo Booth to capture the live camera feed as a movie.

198

3 Click **Take Photo** (⬚).

Note: *You can also press* ⌘+T *or click* **File** *and then click* **Take Photo**.

Photo Booth counts down 3 seconds and then takes the photo.

Note: *When the Mac is taking your picture, be sure to look into the camera, not into the screen.*

Work with Your Photo Booth Picture

D Photo Booth displays the picture.

1 Click the picture.

2 Click **Share** (⬚).

E Click **Add to iPhoto** to add the photo to iPhoto.

F Click **Set Account Picture** to set the photo as your user account picture.

G Click **Set Buddy Picture** to set the photo as your Messages picture.

H Click **Change Twitter Profile Picture** to set the photo as your Twitter avatar.

simplify it

Can I make my photos more interesting?
Definitely. Photo Booth comes with around two dozen special effects. Follow these steps:

1 Click **View**.

2 Click **Show Effects**.

3 Click an icon to select a different page of effects.

A You can also use the arrow buttons to change pages.

4 Click the effect you want to use.

CHAPTER 11

Playing and Creating Digital Video

Your Mac comes with the tools you need to play movies and digital video as well as to create your own digital video movies. Using the iMovie application, you can import camcorder video; apply scene transitions; and add titles, credits, and a soundtrack.

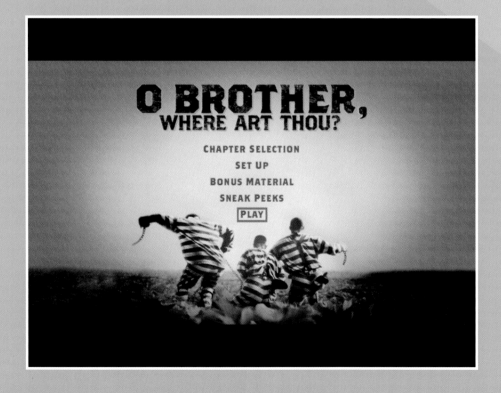

Play a DVD Using DVD Player

If your Mac has a DVD drive, you can insert a DVD movie disc into the drive and then use the DVD Player application to play the movie on your Mac. You can either watch the movie in full-screen mode where the movie takes up the entire Mac screen, or play the DVD in a window while you work on other things. DVD Player has features that enable you to control the movie playback and volume.

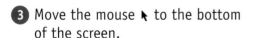

Play a DVD Using DVD Player

Play a DVD Full-Screen

① Insert the DVD disc into your Mac's DVD drive.

DVD Player runs automatically and starts playing the DVD full-screen.

② If you get to the DVD menu, click **Play** to start the movie.

③ Move the mouse ▸ to the bottom of the screen.

The playback controls appear.

Ⓐ Click to pause the movie.

Ⓑ Click to fast-forward the movie.

Ⓒ Click to rewind the movie.

Ⓓ Drag the slider to adjust the volume.

Ⓔ Click to display the DVD menu.

Ⓕ Click to exit full-screen mode.

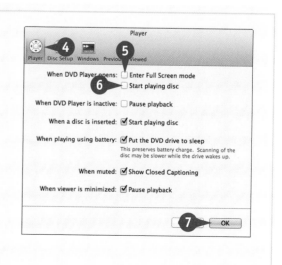

Play a DVD in a Window

1 Insert the DVD disc into your Mac's DVD drive.

DVD Player runs automatically and starts playing the DVD full-screen.

2 Press ⌘+F.

Note: *You can also press* Esc *or move the* ▶ *to the bottom of the screen and then click* **Exit full screen.**

DVD Player displays the movie in a window.

G DVD Player displays the Controller.

3 When you get to the DVD menu, click **Play** to start the movie.

H Click to pause the movie.

I Click and hold to fast-forward the movie.

J Click and hold to rewind the movie.

K Drag the slider to adjust the volume.

L Click to display the DVD menu.

M Click to stop the movie.

N Click to eject the DVD.

---

simplify it

How can I always start my DVDs in a window?

1 Press ⌘+F to switch to the window view.

2 Click **DVD Player** in the menu bar.

3 Click **Preferences** to open the DVD Player preferences.

4 Click the **Player** tab.

5 Click **Enter Full Screen mode** (☑ changes to ☐).

6 If you want to manually control when the playback starts, click **Start playing disc** (☑ changes to ☐).

7 Click **OK** to put the new settings into effect.

Play Digital Video with QuickTime Player

Your Mac comes with an application called QuickTime Player that can play digital video files in various formats. You will mostly use QuickTime Player to play digital video files stored on your Mac, but you can also use the application to play digital video from the web.

QuickTime Player enables you to open video files, navigate the digital video playback, and control the digital video volume. Although you learn only how to play digital video files in this section, the version of QuickTime that comes with OS X 10.8 (Mountain Lion) comes with many extra features, including the ability to record movies and audio and to cut and paste scenes.

Play Digital Video with QuickTime Player

① Click **Finder** (🖼).

② Click **Applications**.

③ Double-click **QuickTime Player** (🔵).

Note: *If you see the QuickTime Player icon in the Dock, you can also click that icon to launch the program.*

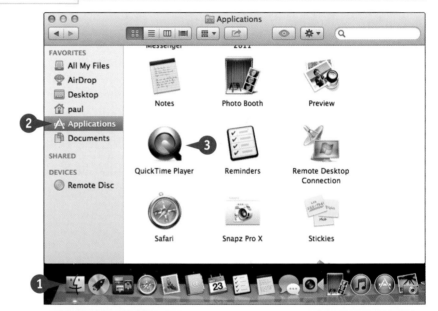

The QuickTime Player application appears.

④ Click **File**.

⑤ Click **Open File**.

Note: *You can also press ⌘+O.*

The Open dialog appears.

6 Locate and click the video file you want to play.

7 Click **Open**.

QuickTime opens a new player window.

8 Click **Play** (▶).

A Click here to fast-forward the video.

B Click here to rewind the video.

C Click and drag this slider to adjust the volume.

If you want to view the video in full-screen mode, press ⌘+F.

simplify it

Can I use QuickTime Player to play a video from the web?
Yes, as long as you know the Internet address of the video, QuickTime Player can play most video formats available on the web. In QuickTime Player, click **File** and then click **Open Location** (or press ⌘+U). In the Open URL dialog, type or paste the video address in the **Movie Location** text box, and then click **Open**.

Create a New Movie Project

The iLife suite installed on your Mac includes iMovie, which enables you to import video from a digital camcorder or video file and use that footage to create your own movies. You do this by first creating a project that holds your video clips, transitions, titles, and other elements of your movie.

When you first start iMovie, the program creates a new project for you automatically. Follow the steps in this section to create subsequent projects. Note, too, that iMovie is also available via the App Store.

Create a New Movie Project

1. Click the **iMovie** icon () in the Dock.

The iMovie window appears.

2. Click **File**.

3. Click **New Project**.

Note: *You can also press* ⌘+N.

The New Project dialog appears.

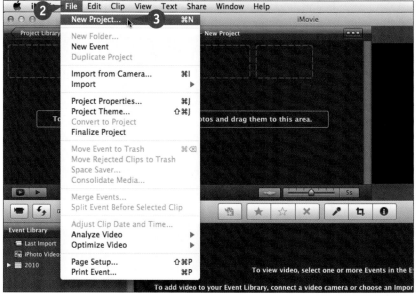

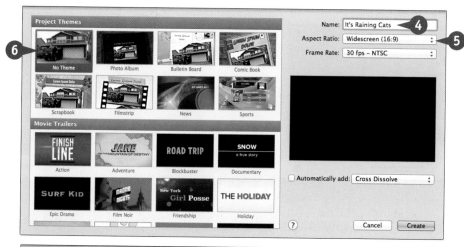

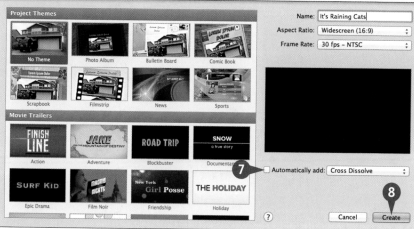

4 In the Name text box, type a name for your project.

5 Click the **Aspect Ratio** ⬍ and then click the ratio you prefer: Widescreen (16:9) or Standard (4:3).

6 To apply a theme to your project, click one in the Project Theme list.

7 To automatically insert transitions between all your clips, click **Automatically add** (☐ changes to ☑) and then click ⬍ to choose the type of transition.

If you chose a theme in Step **6**, the check box changes to **Automatically add transition and titles** by default.

8 Click **Create**.

iMovie creates your new project.

simplify it

What are the iMovie themes?
Each iMovie theme comes with its own set of titles and transitions that are added automatically, saving you a lot of work. There are seven themes in all, including Photo Album, Bulletin Board, and Scrapbook. If a theme is suitable for your project, applying it cuts down on your production time.

How do I switch from one project to another?
You use the Project Library, which is a list of your movie projects. To display it, click **Window** and then click **Show Project Library**. You can also click the **Project Library** button in the top-left corner of the iMovie window. In the Project Library, double-click the project you want to work with.

Import a Video File

With the iMovie application, you can import digital video from a camera for use in your movie project. If you have video content on a USB digital camcorder or smartphone (such as an iPhone 3GS or later), you can connect the device to your Mac and then import some or all of the video to your iMovie project.

If your Mac or monitor has a built-in iSight or FaceTime HD camera, you can also use iMovie to import live images from that camera to use as digital video footage in your movie project.

Import a Video File

Import all Clips

1 Connect the video device to your Mac.

iMovie displays its Import From dialog.

2 Click **Import All**.

iMovie prompts you to create a new event.

3 Click **Create new Event** (☐ changes to ◉).

4 Use the Create new Event text box to type a name for the import event.

Ⓐ If you want to add the video to an existing event, click **Add to existing Event** (☐ changes to ◉) and then choose the event from the pop-up menu.

5 Click **Import**.

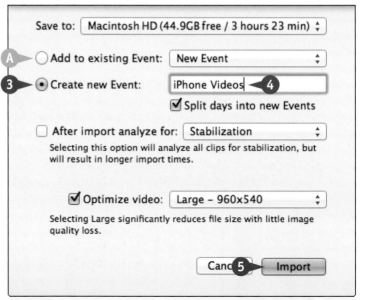

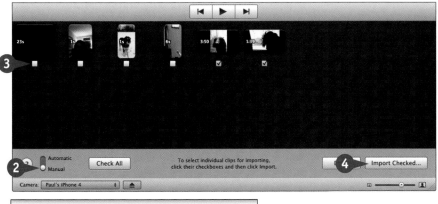

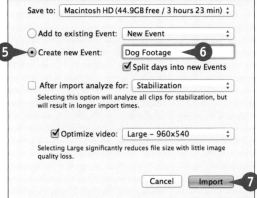

Import Selected Clips

1 Connect the video device to your Mac and place it in playback mode, if necessary.

iMovie displays its Import From dialog.

2 Click **Manual**.

3 Deselect the check box under each clip you do not want to import (☑ changes to ☐).

4 Click **Import Checked**.

iMovie prompts you to create a new event.

5 Click **Create new Event** (☐ changes to ⦿).

6 Use the Create new Event text box to type a name for the import event.

7 Click **Import**.

iMovie begins importing the clips.

8 Click **OK**.

9 Click **Done**.

simplify it

How do I import digital video from my iSight or FaceTime HD camera?
Follow these steps:

1 In iMovie, click **File** and then click **Import from Camera**.

2 Click **Capture**.

3 Follow Steps **5** and **6** in the "Import Selected Clips" section.

4 Click **Capture**.

5 When you are done, click **Stop**.

6 Click **Done**.

Add Video Clips to Your Project

To create and work with a movie project in iMovie, you must first add some video clips to that project. A **video clip** is a segment of digital video. You begin building your movie by adding one or more video clips to your project.

When you import digital video as described in the previous section, iMovie automatically breaks up the video into separate clips, with each clip being the footage shot during a single recording session. You can then decide which of those clips you want to add to your project, or you can add only part of a clip.

Add Video Clips to Your Project

Add an Entire Clip

1. Click the Event Library item that contains the video clip you want to add.

2. Press and hold `Option` and click the clip.

Ⓐ iMovie selects the entire clip.

3. Click and drag the selected clip and drop it in your project at the spot where you want the clip to appear.

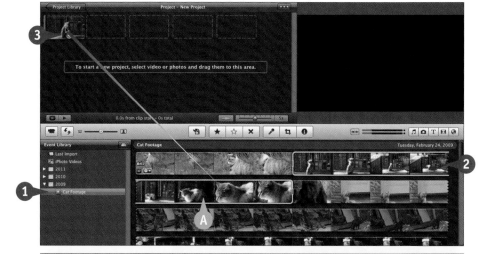

Ⓑ iMovie adds the entire video clip to the project.

Ⓒ iMovie adds an orange bar to the bottom of the original clip to indicate that it has been added to the project.

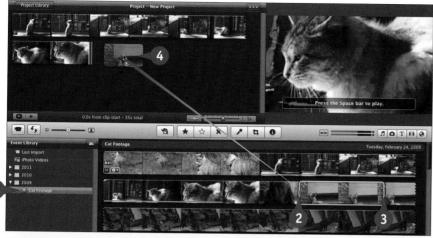

Add a Partial Clip

1 Click the Event Library item that contains the video clip you want to add.

2 Click the clip at the point where you want the selection to begin.

3 Click and drag the right edge of the selection box to the point where you want the selection to end.

4 Click and drag the selected clip and drop it in your project at the spot where you want the clip to appear.

D iMovie adds the selected portion of the video clip to the project.

E iMovie adds an orange bar to the bottom of the original clip to indicate that it has been added to a project.

simplify it

Is it possible to play a clip before I add it?
Yes. The easiest way to do this is to click the clip at the point where you want the playback to start and then press **Spacebar**. iMovie plays the clip in the Viewer in the top-right corner of the window. Press **Spacebar** again to stop the playback.

I added a clip in the wrong place. Can I move it?
Yes. In your project, click the added clip to select it. Use your mouse ▶ to click and drag the clip and then drop the clip in the correct location within the project. If you want to delete the clip from the project, click it, click **Edit**, and then click **Delete Entire Clip** (or press **Option**+**Delete**).

Trim
a Clip

If you have a video clip that is too long or contains footage you do not need, you can shorten the clip or remove the extra footage. Removing parts of a video clip is called *trimming* the clip.

Trimming a clip is particularly useful if you recorded extra, unneeded footage before and after the action you were trying to capture. By trimming this unneeded footage, your movie will include only the scenes you really require.

Trim a Clip

① In your project, click the clip you want to trim.

Ⓐ iMovie selects the entire clip.

② Use your mouse ⬉ to click and drag the left edge of the selection box to the starting position of the part of the clip you want to keep.

③ Use your mouse ⬉ to click and drag the right edge of the selection box to the ending position of the part of the clip you want to keep.

④ Click **Clip**.

⑤ Click **Trim to Selection**.

Note: *You can also press* ⌘+B.

Ⓑ iMovie trims the clip.

Is it possible to trim a certain number of frames from a clip?
Yes, iMovie enables you to trim one frame at a time from either the beginning or the end of the clip. Follow these steps:

① In your project, click the clip you want to trim.

② Click **Clip**.

③ Click **Trim Clip End**.

④ Select the trim direction by clicking **Move Left** or **Move Right**.

⑤ Repeat Step 4 until you reach the number of frames that you want to trim.

Add a Transition between Clips

You can use the iMovie application to enhance the visual appeal of your digital movie by inserting transitions between some or all of the project's video clips. By default, iMovie jumps immediately from the end of one clip to the beginning of the next clip, a transition called a *jump cut*. You can add more visual interest to your movie by adding a transition between the two clips.

iMovie offers 24 different transitions, including various fades, wipes, and dissolves. More transitions are available if you applied a theme to your iMovie project.

Add a Transition between Clips

① Click the **Transitions Browser** button (⊞), or press ⌘+④.

Ⓐ iMovie displays the available transitions.

Note: *To see a preview of a transition, position your mouse ▸ over the transition thumbnail.*

② Use your mouse ▸ to click and drag a transition and drop it between the two clips.

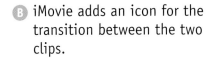

B iMovie adds an icon for the transition between the two clips.

3 Position your mouse ▶ over the beginning of the transition and move the mouse ▶ to the right.

C iMovie displays a preview of the transition.

simplify it

Can I change the duration of the transition?
Yes. The default length is half a second, but you can increase or decrease the duration by following these steps:

1 Double-click the transition icon in your project.

The Inspector appears.

2 Use the Duration text box to set the number of seconds you want the transition to take.

3 If you want to change only the current transition, click **Applies to all transitions** (☑ changes to ☐).

4 Click **Done**.

Add a Photo

You can use the iMovie application to enhance your movie projects with still photos. Although most movie projects consist of several video clips, you can also add a photo to your project. By default, iMovie displays the photo for 4 seconds.

You can also specify how the photo fits in the movie frame: You can adjust the size of the photo to fit the frame, you can crop the photo, or you can apply a Ken Burns effect to animate the static photo, which automatically pans and zooms the photo.

Add a Photo

1 Click the **Photos Browser** button (⬛), or press ⌘+2.

A iMovie displays the available photos.

2 Click the event or album that contains the photo you want to add.

3 Click and drag the photo and drop it inside your project.

B iMovie adds the photo to the movie.

4 Click the photo.

5 Click the **Crop** button (⬛).

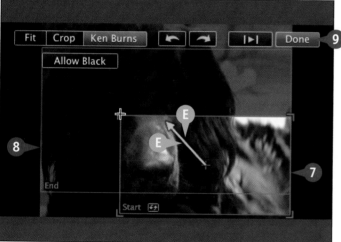

iMovie displays the cropping options for the photo.

⑥ Click **Ken Burns**.

Ⓒ You can also click **Fit** to have iMovie adjust the size of the photo to fit the movie frame.

Ⓓ You can also click **Crop** and then click and drag the cropping rectangle to specify how much of the photo you want to appear in the movie frame.

⑦ Click and drag the green rectangle to set the start point of the Ken Burns animation.

⑧ Click and drag the red rectangle to set the end point of the Ken Burns animation.

Note: *Click and drag the corners and edges of the rectangle to change the size; click and drag the interior of the rectangles to change the position.*

Ⓔ The arrow shows the direction of motion.

⑨ Click **Done**.

---

simplify it

Can I change the length of time that the photo appears in the movie?
Yes. The default length is 4 seconds, but you can increase or decrease the duration by following these steps:

① Double-click the photo in your project.

② Click **Clip**.

③ Use the Duration text box to set the number of seconds you want the photo to appear.

④ To change the duration for all the photos in your project, click **Applies to all stills** (☐ changes to ☑).

⑤ Click **Done**.

Add a Music Track

Using the iMovie application, you can enhance the audio component of your movie by adding one or more songs that play in the background. With iMovie you can also add sound effects and other audio files that you feel would enhance your project's audio track.

To get the best audio experience, you can adjust various sound properties. For example, you can adjust the volume of the music clip or the volume of the video clip. You can also use iMovie to adjust the time it takes for the song clip to fade in and fade out.

Add a Music Track

1 Click the **Music and Sound Effect Browser** button (🎵), or press ⌘+1.

A iMovie displays the available audio files.

2 Click the folder, category, or playlist that contains the track you want to add.

3 Use your mouse ⬉ to click and drag the song and drop it on a video clip.

B iMovie adds the song to the movie.

Note: *iMovie treats the song like a clip, which means you can trim the song as needed, as described earlier in the "Trim a Clip" section.*

4 Double-click the music clip.

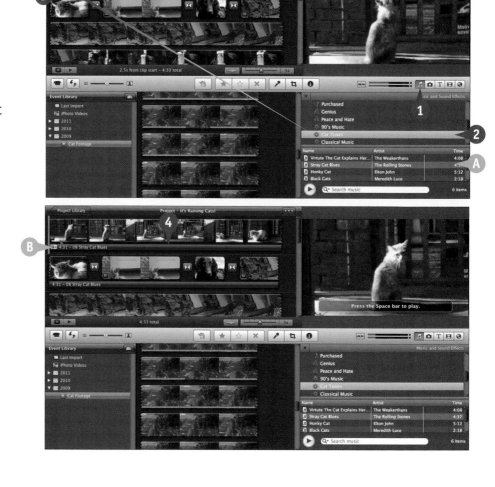

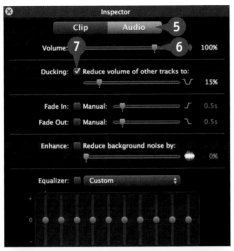

iMovie displays the Inspector.

5 Click the **Audio** tab.

6 Use the **Volume** slider to adjust the volume of the music clip.

7 If you want to reduce the video clip volume, click **Ducking** (☐ changes to ☑) and then click and drag the slider.

8 To adjust the fade-in time, click **Fade In: Manual** (☐ changes to ☑) and then click and drag the slider.

9 To adjust the fade-out time, click **Fade Out: Manual** (☐ changes to ☑) and then click and drag the slider.

10 Click **Done**.

When I add a video clip before the music clip, the music does not play with the new video clip. How can I work around this?
You need to add your song as a background track instead of a clip. Follow these steps:

1 Click 🎵.

2 Click and drag a song onto the project background, not on a clip or between two clips.

A The background turns green when you have the song positioned correctly.

Record a Voiceover

You can use the iMovie application to augment the audio portion of your movie with a voiceover. A *voiceover* is a voice recording that you make using audio equipment attached to your Mac.

A voiceover is useful for explaining a video clip, introducing the movie, or giving the viewer background information about the movie. To record a voiceover, your Mac must have either a built-in microphone, such as the one that comes with the iSight or FaceTime HD camera, or an external microphone connected via an audio jack, USB port, or Bluetooth.

Record a Voiceover

1 If your Mac does not have a built-in microphone, attach a microphone.

Note: *You may need to configure the microphone as the sound input device. Click **System Preferences** (), click **Sound**, click **Input**, and then click your microphone.*

2 Click the **Voiceover** button ().

The Voiceover dialog appears.

3 Click the spot in the movie at which you want the voiceover to begin.

iMovie counts down and
then begins the recording.

4 Speak your voiceover text
into the microphone.

A The progress of the
recording appears here.

5 When you are finished,
click **Recording**.

B iMovie adds the voiceover
to the clip.

6 Click **Close** (⊠).

You can double-click the
voiceover to adjust the
audio, as described in the
previous section.

**Is there a way to tell if my
voice is too loud or too soft?**
Yes, you can use the controls
in the Voiceover dialog to
check your voice level by
talking into the microphone
and then watching the Left
and Right volume meters. Use
the Input Volume slider to
adjust the voice level up or
down, as needed.

A Voice level is too low: No
green bars or just a few
green bars.

B Voice level is too high:
Yellow or red bars.

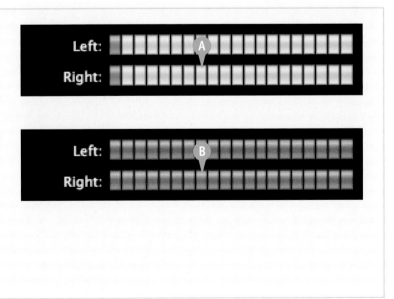

Add Titles and Credits

You can use the iMovie application to enhance your movie project with titles and scrolling credits. You can get your movie off to a proper start by adding a title and a subtitle at or near the beginning of the movie. iMovie offers a number of title styles that you can choose from, and you can also change the title font.

You can also enhance your movie with *scrolling credits*. This is a special type of title that you place at the end of the movie and that scrolls the names of the people responsible for the project.

Add Titles and Credits

① Click the **Titles browser** button (▣).

Ⓐ iMovie displays the available title types.

② Use your mouse ↖ to click and drag a title and drop it where you want the titles to appear.

Note: *To see just the titles, drop the title thumbnail at the beginning of the movie or between two clips. To superimpose the titles on a video clip, drop the title thumbnail on the clip.*

Ⓑ If you want to add credits, click and drag the **Scrolling Credits** thumbnail and drop it at the end of the movie.

C iMovie adds a clip for the title.

3 Replace this text with the movie title.

4 Replace this text with the movie subtitle.

5 Click **Done**.

Note: *iMovie treats the title like a clip, which means you can lengthen or shorten the title duration by clicking and dragging the beginning or end, as described earlier in the "Trim a Clip" section.*

simplify it

How do I change the font of the titles?
The Text menu offers several font-related commands, including Bold, Italic, Bigger, and Smaller. You can also click the **Show Fonts** command to display the Choose Font dialog. If you do not see the Choose Font dialog shown here, you can switch to iMovie's predefined fonts by clicking **iMovie Font Panel**. You can then click a typeface, font color, and type size; click **Done** (**A**) to close the dialog.

Play the Movie

The iMovie application offers the Viewer pane, which you can use to play your movie. While you are building your iMovie project, it is a good idea to occasionally play some or all of the movie to check your progress. For example, you can play the entire movie to make sure the video and audio are working properly and are synchronized correctly. You can also play parts of the movie to ensure that your transitions appear when you want them to.

Play the Movie

Play from the Beginning

1 Click **View**.

2 Click **Play from Beginning**.

Note: *You can also press* (\) *or click the **Play Project from beginning** button (*▶*).*

Play from a Specific Location

1 Position the mouse ▸ over the spot where you want to start playing the movie.

2 Press (Spacebar).

Play a Selection

1 Select the video clips you want to play.

Note: *See the first Tip to learn how to select multiple video clips.*

2 Click **View**.

3 Click **Play Selection**.

Note: *You can also press /.*

How do I select multiple video clips?
To select multiple video clips, press and hold ⌘ and then click anywhere inside each clip you want to select. If you select a clip by accident, ⌘+click it again to deselect it. If you want to skip just a few clips, first press ⌘+A to select all the clips, then press and hold ⌘ and click the clips you do not want in the selection.

Can I enlarge the size of the playback pane?
Yes, you can play your movie in full-screen mode. To do this, click **View** and then click **Play full-screen**. You can also press ⌘+G or click the **Play Project full screen** button (⊙).

Publish Your
Movie to YouTube

When your movie project is complete, you can send it to YouTube for viewing on the web. To publish your movie to YouTube, you must have a YouTube account, available from www.youtube.com. You must also know your YouTube username, which you can see by clicking your account icon on YouTube and then clicking Settings. Your movie must be no more than 15 minutes long. Before you can publish your movie, you must select a YouTube category, such as Entertainment or Pets and Animals, provide a title and description, and enter at least one tag, which is a word or short phrase that describes some aspect of the movie's content.

Publish Your Movie to YouTube

1 Click **Share**.

2 Click **YouTube**.

3 Click **Add**.

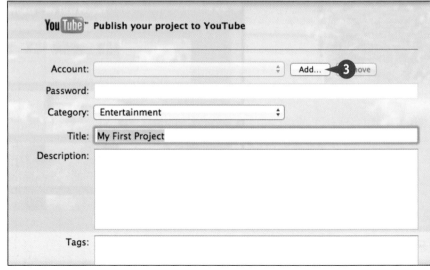

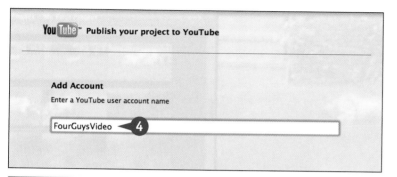

iMovie prompts you for your YouTube username.

④ Type your username.

⑤ Click **Done** (not shown).

⑥ Type your YouTube password.

⑦ Select a category.

⑧ Type a title.

⑨ Type a description.

⑩ Type one or more tags for the video.

⑪ If you do not want to allow anyone to view the movie, click **Make this movie personal** (☑ changes to ☐).

⑫ Click **Next**.

iMovie displays the YouTube terms of service.

⑬ Click **Publish**.

iMovie prepares the movie and then publishes it to YouTube.

⑭ Click **OK** (not shown).

How do I publish my movie to Facebook?
If you have a Facebook account, click **Share** and then click **Facebook**. Click **Add**, type your Facebook e-mail address, and then click **Done**. Type your Facebook password. Use the **Viewable by** pop-up to choose who can see the video, such as Only Friends or Everyone. Type a title and description, select a size, click **Next**, and then click **Publish**.

How do I view my movie outside of iMovie?
Beyond viewing it on YouTube or Facebook, you need to export the movie to a digital video file. Click **Share** and then click **Export Movie** (or press ⌘+E). Type a title for the movie, and then click a **Size to Export** option, such as Large or HD 720p (☐ changes to ◉). Click **Export**.

CHAPTER 12

Customizing OS X to Suit Your Style

OS X comes with a number of features that enable you to customize your Mac. For example, you might not like the default desktop background or the layout of the Dock. Not only can you change the appearance of OS X to suit your taste, but you can also change the way OS X works to make it easier and more efficient for you to use.

Display System Preferences

You can find many of the OS X customization features in System Preferences, a collection of settings and options that control the overall look and operation of OS X. You can use System Preferences to change the desktop background, specify a screen saver, set your Mac's sleep options, add user accounts, and customize the Dock, to name some of the tasks that you learn about in this chapter. To use these settings, you must know how to display the System Preferences window.

Display System Preferences

Open System Preferences

1 In the Dock, click **System Preferences** (⬚).

The System Preferences window appears.

Customizing OS X to Suit Your Style

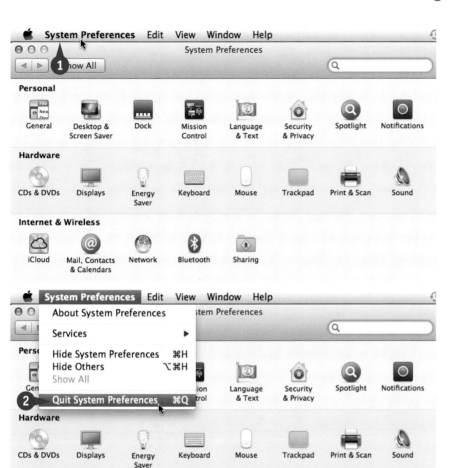

Close System Preferences

1 Click **System Preferences**.

2 Click **Quit System Preferences**.

Sometimes when I open System Preferences, I do not see all the icons. How can I restore the original icons?

When you click an icon in System Preferences, the window changes to show just the options and settings associated with that icon. To return to the main System Preferences window, click **View** and then click **Show All Preferences** (or press ⌘+🇱) or use either of the following techniques:

A Click ◄ until the main window appears.

B Click **Show All**.

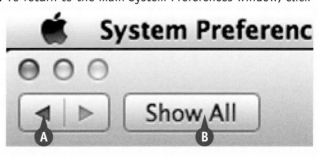

Change the Desktop Background

To give OS X a different look, you can change the default desktop background. OS X offers a wide variety of desktop background options. For example, OS X comes with several dozen images you can use, from abstract patterns to photos of plants and other natural images. You can also choose a solid color as the desktop background, or you can use one of your own photos. You can change the desktop background to show either a fixed image or a series of images that change periodically.

Change the Desktop Background

Set a Fixed Background Image

1 Open System Preferences.

Note: *See the "Display System Preferences" section, earlier in this chapter.*

2 Click **Desktop & Screen Saver**.

Note: *You can also right-click the desktop and then click Change Desktop Background.*

The desktop and screen saver preferences appear.

3 Click **Desktop**.

4 Click the image category you want to use.

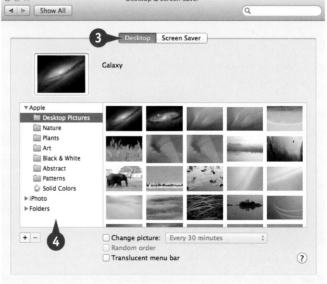

5 Click the image you want to use as the desktop background.

Your Mac changes the desktop background.

6 If you chose a photo in Step **5**, click ⊟ and then click an option from the pop-up menu to determine how your Mac displays the photo.

Note: *Another way to set a fixed background image is to select a photo in iPhoto, click **Share**, and then click **Set Desktop**.*

Set a Changing Background Image

1 Click **Change picture** (☐ changes to ☑).

2 Click ⊟ in the pop-up menu and then click how often you want the background image to change.

3 If you want your Mac to choose the periodic image randomly, click **Random order** (☐ changes to ☑).

Your Mac changes the desktop background periodically based on your chosen interval.

When I choose a photo, how do the various options differ for displaying the photo?
Your Mac gives you five options for displaying the photo:

- **Fill Screen.** This option expands the photo by the same amount in all four directions until it fills the entire desktop.

- **Fit to Screen.** This option expands the photo in all four directions until the photo is the same height or the same width as the desktop.

- **Stretch to Fill Screen.** This option expands the photo in all four directions until it fills the entire desktop.

- **Center.** This option displays the photo at its actual size in the center of the desktop.

- **Tile.** This option repeats your photo multiple times to fill the entire desktop.

Activate the Screen Saver

You can set up OS X to display a *screen saver*, a moving pattern or series of pictures. The screen saver appears after your computer has been idle for a while. If you leave your monitor on for long stretches while your computer is idle, a faint version of the unmoving image can endure for a while on the screen, a phenomenon known as *persistence*. A screen saver prevents this by displaying a moving image. However, persistence is not a major problem for modern screens, so for the most part you use a screen saver for visual interest.

Activate the Screen Saver

1 Open System Preferences.

Note: *See the "Display System Preferences" section, earlier in this chapter.*

2 Click **Desktop & Screen Saver**.

The desktop and screen saver preferences appear.

3 Click **Screen Saver**.

4 Click the screen saver you want to use.

A A preview of the screen saver appears here.

5 Click the **Start after** and then click a time delay until the screen saver begins.

Note: *The interval you choose is the number of minutes or hours that your Mac must be idle before the screen saver starts.*

B If the screen saver is customizable, click **Screen Saver Options** to configure it.

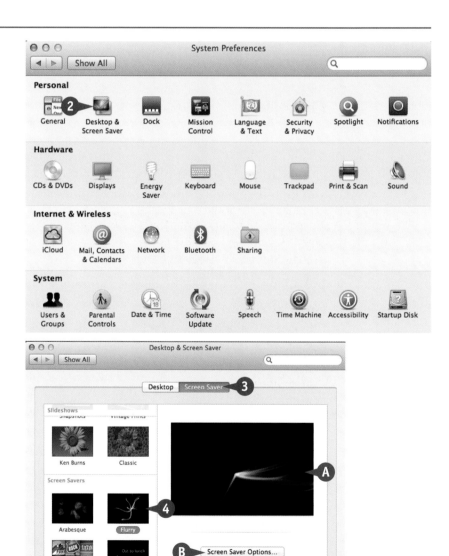

C If you chose a slide show instead of a screen saver, click the **Source** ⊟ to select an image collection.

D If you also want to see the current time when the screen saver is active, click **Show with clock** (☐ changes to ☑).

---

simplify it

What are hot corners and how do I configure them?

A *hot corner* is a corner of your Mac's screen that you have set up to perform some action when you move the mouse ⬑ to that corner. To configure hot corners, follow these steps:

1 Follow Steps **1** to **4** to select a screen saver.

2 Click **Hot Corners**.

System Preferences displays the Active Screen Corners dialog.

3 In the top-left pop-up menu, click ⊟ and then click the action you want to perform when you move ⬑ to the top-left corner of the screen.

4 Click ⊟ and then click the action you want to perform when you move ⬑ to the top-right corner of the screen.

5 Click ⊟ and then click the action you want to perform when you move ⬑ to the bottom-left corner of the screen.

6 Click ⊟ and then click the action you want to perform when you move ⬑ to the bottom-right corner of the screen.

7 Click **OK**.

Active Screen Corners

3 ▸ Start Screen Saver   Put Display to Sleep ◂ **4**

5 ▸ Dashboard   Desktop ◂ **6**

7 ▸ OK

Set Your Mac's Sleep Options

You can make OS X more energy efficient by configuring parts of your Mac to go into sleep mode automatically when you are not using them. *Sleep mode* means that your display or your Mac is in a temporary low-power mode. This saves energy on all Macs, and also saves battery power on a notebook

Mac. For example, you can set up OS X to put the display to sleep automatically after a period of inactivity. Similarly, you can configure OS X to put your entire Mac to sleep after you have not used it for a specified amount of time.

Set Your Mac's Sleep Options

Open the Energy Saver Preferences

1 Open System Preferences.

Note: *See the "Display System Preferences" section, earlier in this chapter.*

2 Click **Energy Saver**.

The Energy Saver preferences appear.

Set Sleep Options for a Desktop Mac

1 Click and drag ☐ to set the computer sleep timer.

This specifies the period of inactivity after which your computer goes to sleep.

2 Click and drag ☐ to set the display sleep timer.

This specifies the period of inactivity after which your display goes to sleep.

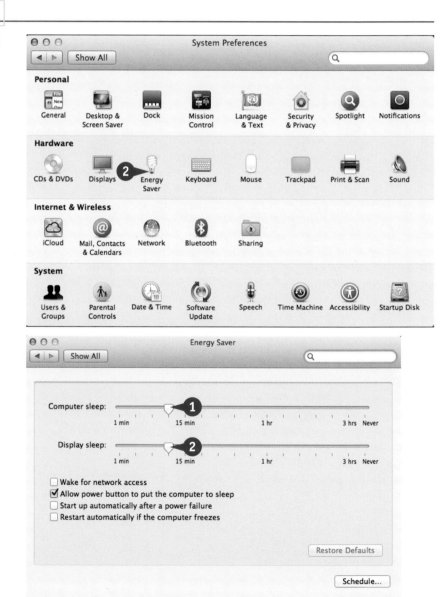

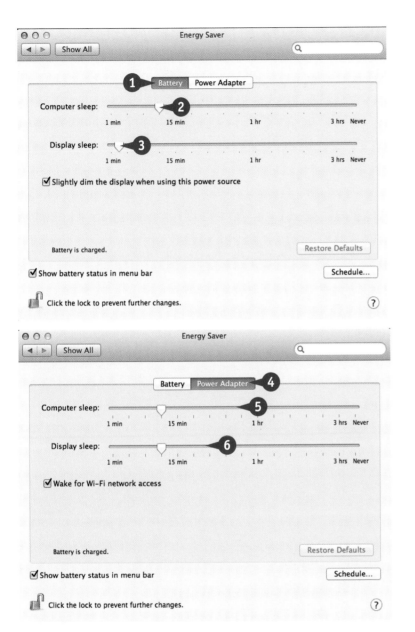

Set Sleep Options for a Notebook Mac

1 Click **Battery**.

2 Click and drag ☐ to set the computer sleep timer for when your Mac is on battery power.

3 Click and drag ☐ to set the display sleep timer for when your Mac is on battery power.

4 Click **Power Adapter**.

5 Click and drag ☐ to set the computer sleep timer for when your Mac is plugged in.

6 Click and drag ☐ to set the display sleep timer for when your Mac is plugged in.

---

simplify it

After changing the display sleep timer, why can I not see my screen saver?
You have set the display sleep timer to a time that is less than your screen saver timer. For example, suppose you have configured OS X to switch on the screen saver after 15 minutes. If you then set the display sleep timer to a shorter interval, such as 10 minutes, OS X will always put the display to sleep before the screen saver appears. To avoid this, set the display sleep timer longer than your screen saver timer.

Change the Display Resolution

You can change the resolution of the OS X display. This enables you to adjust the display for best viewing or for maximum compatibility with whatever application you are using.

Increasing the display resolution is an easy way to create more space on the screen for applications and windows, because the objects on the screen appear smaller. Conversely, if you are having trouble reading text on the screen, decreasing the display resolution can help, because the screen objects appear larger. You can change the OS X display resolution using either the System Preferences window or the menu bar.

Change the Display Resolution

Change Resolution via the Display Preferences

1 Open System Preferences.

Note: *See the "Display System Preferences" section, earlier in this chapter.*

2 Click **Displays**.

The Displays preferences appear.

3 Click **Display**.

4 Click the resolution you want to use.

Your Mac adjusts the screen to the new resolution.

Ⓐ To change the resolution using your Mac's menu bar, as described next, click **Show mirroring options in menu bar when available** (☐ changes to ☑).

Change Resolution via the Menu Bar

1 Click the **Mirroring Options** icon ().

Your Mac opens a menu that shows the most commonly or recently used resolutions.

B The resolution with the check mark (☑) is the current resolution.

2 Click the resolution you want to use.

Your Mac adjusts the screen to the new resolution.

What do the resolution numbers mean?
The resolution numbers are expressed in *pixels*, short for picture elements, which are the individual dots that make up what you see on your Mac's screen. The pixels are arranged in rows and columns, and the resolution tells you the number of pixels in each row and column. So a resolution of 1024 x 768 means that the display is using 1,024 pixel rows and 768 pixel columns.

Create an App Folder in Launchpad

You can make Launchpad easier to work with by combining two or more icons into a single storage area called an *app folder*. OS X Mountain Lion displays the Launchpad icons in up to five rows per screen, with up to seven icons in each row, so you can have as many as 35 icons in each Launchpad screen. Also, if you have configured your Mac with a relatively low display resolution, you might see only partial app names in the Launchpad screens.

All of this can make it difficult to locate the app you want. However, by creating app folders, you can organize similar apps and reduce the clutter on the Launchpad screens.

Create an App Folder in Launchpad

1 Click **Launchpad** (⬚).

A Launchpad displays icons for each installed application.

2 Click the dot for the Launchpad screen you want to work with.

3 Use the mouse ⬚ to click and drag an icon that you want to include in the folder, and drop it on another icon that you want to include in the same folder.

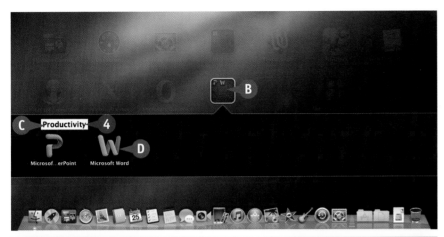

Ⓑ Launchpad creates the app folder.

Ⓒ Launchpad applies a name to the folder based on the type of applications in the folder.

Ⓓ Launchpad adds the icons to the app folder.

④ To specify a different name, click the name and then type the one you prefer.

⑤ Click the Launchpad screen, outside of the app folder.

Ⓔ Launchpad displays the app folder.

⑥ To add more icons to the new app folder, use the mouse ➤ to click and drag each icon and drop it on the folder.

Note: *To launch a program from an app folder, click 🔘, click the app folder to open it, and then click the program's icon.*

simplify it

Can I make changes to an app folder once it has been created?
Yes, you can rename the folder or rearrange the icons within the folder. To get started, click 🔘 to open Launchpad, and then click the app folder to open it. To rename the app folder, click the current name, type the new name, and then press Return . To rearrange the icons, use the mouse ➤ to drag and drop the apps within the folder. When you are done, click outside the app folder to close it.

Add a User Account

You can share your Mac with another person by creating a user account for that person. This enables the person to log on to OS X and use the system. The new user account is completely separate from your own account. This means that the other person can change settings, create documents, and perform other OS X tasks without interfering with your own settings or data. For maximum privacy for all users, you should set up each user account with a password.

Add a User Account

1 Open System Preferences.

Note: *See the "Display System Preferences" section, earlier in this chapter.*

2 Click **Users & Groups**.

A In most OS X systems, to modify accounts you must click the **Lock** icon (🔒) and then enter your administrator password (🔒 changes to 🔓).

3 Click **Add** (➕).

The New Account dialog appears.

④ Click ⊟ and then click an account type.

⑤ Type the user's name.

⑥ Edit the short username that OS X creates.

⑦ Type a password for the user.

⑧ Retype the user's password.

⑨ As an option, type a hint that OS X will display if the user forgets the password.

⑩ Click **Create User**.

Ⓑ OS X adds the user account to the Users & Groups preferences window.

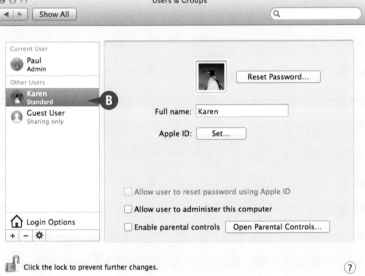

Which account type should I use for the new account?
The Standard account type is a good choice because it can make changes only to its own account settings. Avoid the Administrator option because it is a powerful account type that enables the user to make major changes to the system. If the user is a child, consider the Managed with Parental Controls account type, which enables you to place restrictions on the user's actions and on the content the person can view.

Index

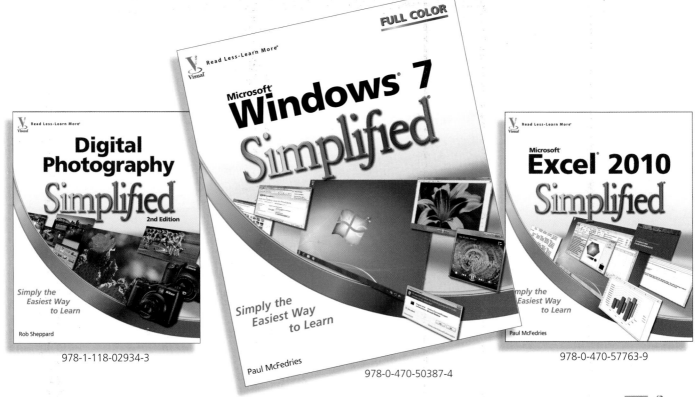